30 STEPS
TO
BECOMING
A WRITER

30 STEPS TO BECOMING A WRITER

by SCOTT EDELSTEIN

Introduction by Natalie Goldberg

RUNNING PRESS
PHILADELPHIA • LONDON

9   8   7   6   5   4   3   2   1
Digit on the right indicates the number of this printing

Library of Congress Catalog Number: 2005924487

ISBN 0-7624-1960-1
Interior design by Jan Greenberg
Edited by Jennifer Kasius

This book may be ordered by mail from the publisher. Please include $2.50 for
postage and handling.
But try your bookstore first!

Running Press Book Publishers
125 South Twenty-second Street
Philadelphia, Pennsylvania 19103-4399

Visit us on the web!
www.runningpress.com

TABLE OF CONTENTS

INTRODUCTION

Stepping Into Clarity

by Natalie Goldberg

Author of *Writing Down the Bones* and *Wild Mind*

I'd like to propose a first step before you begin *30 Steps to Becoming a Writer*: that you believe this book.

I've just finished writing my tenth one, this time a memoir (I've tried all forms). And in reading Scott I am amazed that he can harness the writer's process so simply and elegantly. No room for hysterics, moaning, running to a psychiatrist to discuss your writer's block, no dreaming forever. This is solid advice, a real foothold into the writer's mind.

He even begins by listing the tools necessary for the task. Just like a carpenter, an electrician. There is something comforting about the material world. We are grounded in our equipment.

Then follows no-nonsense instructions in setting up your workplace. This is realistic, sound advice. Pay attention.

I love particularly the way Scott delineates the journal and the writer's notebook. I will never be confused again. And I know it is a point of perplexity for my writing students: What's the difference? Where do I write what? In this book we can all find a clear answer.

So now, no excuses. Heed Scott's advice and get to work.

—Natalie Goldberg

PREFACE

What Makes This Book Different— and How It Can Help

How many times have you said to yourself, "I'd like to write" or "I wish I could become a writer"? How often have you dreamed of putting your ideas and feelings on paper—perhaps to be published and shared with others? And how many times have you met other writers, or read their work, and yearned to do what they do?

If the answer to any of the above questions is "more than once," then this book is for you.

Plenty of people *want* to become writers, and many of them want to publish what they write. But many of them simply haven't known what to do to turn their dreams and desires into reality—or even how to get started in the first place. Perhaps you're one of these people yourself.

The problem is that, until now, no book has offered prospective writers a complete step-by-step program for attaining their goals and fulfilling their dreams.

Certainly there are plenty of writers' courses, conferences, and workshops available, as well as many writers' magazines, hundreds of books on writing, and innumerable websites for writers. Many of these can be quite useful. In fact, I've written several such books myself, including one for beginners, *The No-Experience-Necessary Writer's Course.*

But for all of their good advice and practical tips, none of these resources charts a clear, step-by-step course for becoming a writer.

30 Steps to Becoming a Writer isn't like any of these other sources of information and inspiration. It's based on a single essential premise: that you can learn to write moving and successful stories, essays, poems, and other pieces by following a series of specific steps and instructions. Furthermore, you can use the same kind of step-by-step procedure to help get your work published in magazines, newspapers, websites, and other media.

It's possible to learn to sing a beautiful ballad, knit an exquisite sweater, or grow a spectacular garden by following clear, careful, step-by-step instructions. Why should writing be any different?

The answer, of course, is that it isn't. And it is just such a step-by-step approach that makes this book unique—and so practical, helpful, and effective.

30 Steps to Becoming a Writer offers you a consistent, well-planned program that takes you through 30 clearly-delineated steps, each one designed to help you grow as a writer. By the time you've completed all 30 of these steps, you'll not only have finished several different pieces of writing, but you'll have submitted at least one of them to editors for possible publication. Furthermore, you'll have become a practicing writer with some real experience, some completed works in your portfolio, and some professional success—or, at the very least, professional aspirations. Best of all, in the process you'll have learned how to continue developing your writing skills on your own.

In short, you'll have attained your goal of becoming a writer. You'll be doing what, in the past, you only wished, dreamed, or hoped you could do. (And if you've bought this book as part of *The Complete Writer's Kit*, you'll be able to go further still by following the additional steps in the mini-book *Get Published in 6 Months or Less*.)

You don't need any special experience in order to follow this program. You don't have to have a college degree in English, or be an avid reader of great literature (or anything else). You don't need to have taken courses in creative writing, and you don't need lots of writing experience under your belt. All you need is a desire to express yourself in words.

Writing is and always will be a creative, intuitive, and sometimes mysterious process. Following a series of clearly-defined steps doesn't change this a bit. Indeed, some of what you write as you follow this program will surprise (and often delight) you. You may discover things about who you are and what is important to you that you didn't know before. And that's wonderful. Each new insight can take you deeper into your own writing—and teach you more about yourself and the world.

You may be wondering about my own background and experience as a writer, so I'll tell you. I started writing seriously as a teenager and have been doing it ever since—for over 30 years now. I've published more than 120 short stories and articles in magazines and anthologies around the world. I've also published over a dozen books, including several specifically for writers. I've worked as a journalist; a magazine columnist; an arts reviewer; a writer for businesses, nonprofit organizations, and government; a writing and publishing consultant; a literary agent; a ghostwriter; a college-level writing teacher; and an editor for book, magazine, and newspaper publishers. What's most important of all, though, is this: I love writing, and I enjoy helping others to reach their own writing goals. I do this through teaching, through the books I've published on the art and craft of writing, and through one-on-one consultations with writers and writers-to-be.

My hope is that you will use this book to help you to reach your own writing goals—and to make your dream of becoming a writer come true.

One last word: if you know of someone else who has talked about wanting to become a writer, but who hasn't yet gotten started, please consider giving them this book as a gift—or loaning them your copy. You could be helping the next Mark Twain or Toni Morrison launch their writing career.

— Scott Edelstein
Minneapolis

PART 1

Getting Started

STEP 1

Acquire the Basic Tools and Resources

One of the best things about writing is that it doesn't require expensive equipment. For centuries writers have gotten by with nothing more than pens and paper. Today it is still possible to be a writer with only these two low-tech tools (which remain as reliable, useful, and effective as ever).

Indeed, in the 21st century, many writers still choose to do much or all of their writing in longhand, and use a computer only for typing up, storing, and printing finished manuscripts.

Let's start with these two humblest but most essential tools.

WRITING IMPLEMENTS. Most writers have strong preferences here. This is true even of writers who compose on computers and use pens or pencils only to make corrections and notes. Some considerations include:

- **Aesthetics.** Do you prefer something beautiful and personal, or something cheap and easily replaceable? Do you want a writing implement that makes a statement? That clearly reflects who you are? That has your name printed on it? Or do you want something utilitarian that simply feels good in your hand? Do you want to use the same, familiar pen whenever you write? Or, like me, do you want something you can grab quickly, leave behind, and replace with ease?

- **Pen vs. pencil.** Do you want something easily erasable or something more permanent? What looks and feels better to you, lead or ink?

- **Weight and heft.** Do you like something heavy and substantial, or light and very easy to move?
- **Diameter and grip.** Pens and pencils can be narrow or thick, smooth or rough, rounded or many-sided.
- **Ink style.** Do you prefer ink cartridges? Ballpoint refills? Narrow-tipped markers? Pencils with replaceable lead? Throwaway ballpoints? Pencils that you can sharpen down to nubs?
- **Point width.** My wife thinks fine-point pens are sophisticated. I prefer medium points; fine points feel wimpy to me.
- **Ink color.** I use only black ink. Poet John Sorrell uses half a dozen different-colored pens, each color signifying a different draft or purpose.
- **Color.** Should your pen (not the ink, but the pen itself) be a color that reflects who you are? Or do you prefer clear, non-refillable ballpoints so that you can see exactly how much ink is left?

PAPER. I have a strong preference for white unlined 8½×11 inch single sheets. Several writers I know prefer lined legal pads (some like yellow; others prefer white). Natalie Goldberg uses 8×10 spiral notebooks. Still other writers use bound blank books, typically 5×8 or 6×9.

You don't have to use paper at all when you write, of course. Some writers create their initial drafts by dictating into tape recorders, or use voice recognition programs such as Naturally Speaking.

Although you can create your work on any kind of paper you please, final manuscripts and professional correspondence should be printed on 8½×11 unlined white paper, without holes. I recommend 20-pound paper, which is available from office supply stores and catalogs for $3 to $4 per ream (500 sheets). Final manuscripts and letters should always be prepared on a computer printer using dark black ink and 10- to 14-point type. (Complete details on preparing a manuscript appear in Step 26.)

COMPUTER. A computer is a good investment for almost any writer (yes, even poets). New, up-to-date systems (including color monitors and laser printers) are available for under $500 from retailers such as www.pcmall.com (800-555-6255), www.pcconnection.com (888-213-0260), www.jandr.com (800-806-1115), and www.compusa.com (800-266-7872). Most systems come with Microsoft Word, WordPerfect, Microsoft Works, or AppleWorks. All of these work well, and all can read and work with files created by the other three. If you do have to buy your own word processing software, get Microsoft Works, which is versatile and inexpensive.

If you can't afford a low-end laser printer (cost: $100), settle for an inkjet printer (cost: under $50). If you can't afford any computer at all, remember that libraries have computers and printers available at no charge.

If you're not sure yet whether you do your best composing with a pen or pencil, a computer, a tape recorder or voice recognition program, or even a typewriter, experiment with each. Some writers find the kinesthetic movements of writing in longhand essential to composing; others find inspiration in the clacking of typewriter keys, or the appearance of words on a screen, or the sound of their own voice speaking to them.

Other basic tools I strongly recommend:

- A thick dictionary, preferably unabridged. Any large American dictionary will do. (I don't recommend the *Oxford English Dictionary*, since it follows British conventions and usage.)
- A thick thesaurus. This is a book that lists synonyms (words with similar or identical definitions). Get a thesaurus arranged alphabetically rather than by subject.
- An easy-to-use guide to the rules and conventions of English.

My own favorite is *The Gregg Reference Manual* by William A. Sabin. Also good is *A Writer's Reference* by Diana Hacker.

- Erasers (both pencil and ink).
- Paper clips (regular and jumbo).
- Butterfly clamps (large paper clips shaped like butterflies, for holding large manuscripts together).
- File folders; a place to keep them (a cardboard box or milk crate will do); and a simple system for organizing them (e.g., alphabetically).
- Typing paper (white, unlined, 8½x11 inch, without holes) for manuscripts and business letters.
- Plain white business (#10) envelopes.
- Large (9×12 or 10×13) envelopes, white or manila, for mailing out manuscripts.
- Blank mailing labels (about 1×3" each).
- Blank floppy disks and/or CDs.

The following are not strictly necessary, but can be very useful:

- A good, sturdy stapler.
- Staples.
- Rubber bands.
- A 12-inch ruler.
- A tax record book, for keeping track of your writing expenses and income.

The best prices on office supplies come from catalog office supply dealers such as Reliable (800-735-4000, www.reliable.com), Viking (800-711-4242, www.viking.com), Office Max (800-283- 7674, www.officemax.com), Office Depot (800-463-3768, www.officedepot.com), and Staples (800-378-2753, www.staples.com). Depending on where you live, there may be no state tax and/or no shipping charges—and everything you need is delivered directly to your door, usually in 2-3 days.

YOUR ASSIGNMENT: Purchase (or otherwise acquire) two or three of the right pens, a supply of your preferred paper, and everything on the list of basic items in this chapter. Also get any of the items in the "very useful" list that you feel will genuinely help you as a writer.

Once you own these items, you've completed Step 1. Now it's time for you to find and set up a regular place to write.

STEP 2

Set Up a Place to Work

In order to do your best work, it's important that you locate or create a place—or several places—where you can write comfortably and productively.

Different writers require vastly different work environments. Some like to be surrounded by activity or sound; others prefer solitude and quiet. Jane Austen was able to write while family conversation went on all around her; Virginia Woolf, on the other hand, felt it essential to have a quiet, separate, private space set aside specifically for her writing.

Whatever your needs and preferences, the question to ask yourself is this: what feels comfortable, yet helps me to remain alert and focused?

For many writers, the answer is a coffee shop or restaurant, a library, or some other public place where they can sit and work—alone, yet in the midst of other people. For others, the ideal location might be a park bench, or a rocking chair on the back porch, or the base of a favorite tree.

Some writers need a distinctly private space where they can control the level of noise and activity. For these people, a spot that is all their own, at least for certain scheduled hours, is essential. This doesn't necessarily have to be a separate room. Often a corner of the dining room or bedroom will do. Sometimes a library study carrel, or a cubicle during non-business hours, is sufficient.

Still other writers have two, three, or even more different places where they write, depending on their mood, their needs, and the circumstances of the moment.

Whatever location you choose, be sure that you arrange it as much to your liking as possible. Here are some basics to consider:

- **Lighting.** Do you prefer a single bright halogen lamp? Daylight shining over your shoulder? Utter darkness except for your monitor, even in the daytime? A full-spectrum lamp?
- **Temperature.** Are you most comfortable with a blanket over your lap? A heating pad on your shoulder? A breeze blowing on your bare feet?
- **Back support.** Are you most comfortable sitting in a straight-backed chair? Relaxing in a recliner? (I kneel on a kneeling bench in front of my computer; without it, my back would grow stiff and painful very quickly.) Remember that what works best for someone else may not work for you. Mark Twain and Truman Capote did much of their writing lying in bed; I've tried it a few times, and each time I quickly fell asleep.
- **The proper height and angles for your wrist and writing arm.** Some people use a wrist rest; some use a writing board; a few ambidextrous writers switch hands from time to time.

If you need or prefer quiet, find a place to work where you can shut the door and windows. If this simply isn't possible, wear earplugs, or play a tape or CD of the ocean, or hook up a white noise generator. Unplug your phone while you work, or turn off its ringer, or move it to another room.

If you're like many writers, you may prefer to have music, or even news or talk shows, playing in the background as you write. If this describes you, have the appropriate equipment set up and ready to use, and keep a selection of tapes, CDs, or DVDs nearby.

If you need or prefer privacy, being able to close (and perhaps lock) your door is essential, particularly if you have kids. Or, set up your workspace in a part of your home where people rarely go, such as the attic or garage. Another option is to rent a room or other space entirely outside of your home. If none of these arrangements is possible, try setting your workspace apart with a folding screen.

No matter what your physical setup, you can only have privacy if other people let you alone. Make a clear agreement with other members of your household that at certain specified times you are not to be disturbed, except in genuine emergencies. If anyone violates that agreement, shoo them out promptly and firmly, and insist that they honor the privacy agreement in the future. (If you have kids, they may test these limits repeatedly; if you are not firm about respecting this boundary, they may completely erode your privacy. Don't be afraid to hang a sign on the door that says "Do Not Disturb Until _____.")

Keep extra paper, pens, other supplies, frequently-used books and important files where they can be easily reached. Keep everything well organized, so that you can quickly find whatever you need.

Thus far I've been discussing practical considerations; now let's turn to some aesthetic ones.

If possible, try to find or arrange a spot that has a pleasant view, but not so pleasant that it distracts you from your writing. (The late writer Isaac Asimov insisted on working in a windowless room with bare white walls, so that nothing would draw him away from his writing.) If you like, decorate your workspace so that it's inviting and inspiring. Keep a pot of coffee, or a cooler of soft drinks, or a jar full of pretzels nearby. Type up some inspiring quotes and tape them to the wall next to you.

If you write in more than one place, it is an excellent idea to make one spot your home base. This might be the place where you do most of your writing, or it may simply be the spot where you keep all of your supplies and writing-related files.

The same principles of comfort and functionality apply to how you dress when you write. Wear what feels good, keeps you sufficiently warm or cool, and doesn't restrict the movements of your arms, hand, or fingers. In the winter I have done much of my writing in my bathrobe; in the summer I often wear nothing but a pair of swimming trunks. Some writers wear a particular outfit whenever they write, one that makes them feel especially comfortable or productive or inspired.

In addition to setting up your workspace, you may want to establish a regular pre-writing ritual. I don't mean something religious or spiritual (though you can include these elements in your ritual if you like), but a quick routine that gets you in the mood to write. For example, you might begin each writing session by getting a cup of coffee and calling over your dog; or you might sharpen a pencil and reread the previous day's work; or you might put on your favorite slippers, do fifty jumping jacks, and select a CD to listen to while you write.

Whatever ritual you devise, be sure that it takes no more than ten minutes. Remember, its purpose is to warm you up and get you in the mood to write, not to help you put off getting started.

Is a pre-writing ritual necessary for every writer? Not really. If you can get yourself in the right frame of mind by simply sitting down and picking up your pen—or turning on your computer—then those two simple actions can serve as the only pre-writing ritual you will need.

Lastly, you may find that writing at certain times, or according to a pre-planned schedule, helps you to be more inspired or productive. A schedule can help to keep you focused and on track, and beginners in particular often need the extra dose of motivation that a schedule can provide.

Observe your own body rhythms. When are you most alert and energetic? (For many people, this is early morning, late evening, or both.) To the extent possible, try to schedule your writing sessions for times when you are at your best.

A schedule also enables you to declare to others that during certain hours you cannot be disturbed. And if you're a busy person who must plan your leisure time in advance, a writing schedule is absolutely essential.

If you're like many writers, you'll need to schedule your writing times around the rhythms of your family or household rather than (or in addition to) those of your own body. That's fine. Remind yourself that hundreds of important books have been written in the early mornings and late evenings, while writers' families have slumbered peacefully nearby.

YOUR ASSIGNMENT: Find one or more places where you can write comfortably and productively. If you pick more than one, designate one as your home base.

Prepare each writing site to be as pleasant and functional as possible. Pay attention to lighting, posture, temperature, privacy, and noise level. Then, unless you'll be writing in a public place, add some personal extras—photographs, flowers, posters, a tea kettle, a portable CD player, inspiring quotes, etc.—to make your workplace even more comfortable and attractive.

Set up your desk or other writing surface, and arrange all the supplies and materials you'll need so they are close at hand.

If you like, devise a pre-writing ritual that helps you to make a smooth and effective transition from your everyday life to the one-pointedness of writing.

If you feel it will be helpful, set up a schedule of writing sessions, and make agreements with other household members about when you are to be left undisturbed. Stick to those agreements. As the weeks pass, adjust your schedule as necessary.

Congratulations on completing Step 2. You've laid the groundwork for productive and successful writing by establishing a spot that's yours and yours alone—one that's designed to most nurture your writing.

STEP 3

Begin a Writer's Notebook

A writer's notebook is a place to record ideas, observations, anecdotes, images, outlines, descriptions, notes, and other raw material for your writing. Although most writers keep a notebook of some sort, there are probably as many different ways to keep one as there are writers alive.

A writer's notebook is different from a journal or diary, where you record your thoughts, feelings, and concerns. A journal is a strictly personal undertaking, a volume about yourself that you keep for yourself. In contrast, a writer's notebook exists to support *your writing,* and to provide material and inspiration for it.

I don't mean to suggest that you shouldn't keep a journal in addition to a writer's notebook if you wish. In fact, many writers regularly write in both, or merge the two into a single volume. That's fine, so long as you don't neglect the purposes of a writer's notebook described above.

Some writers organize their notebooks chronologically, as in a diary. Others divide up their notebooks according to subject. For instance, you might break up your notebook into sections pertaining to the different pieces you're working on—e.g., Ghost Poem, Kidnapping Story, Highway Editorial, Book Proposal, etc. Or, if you're a fiction writer, you might separate your notebook into sections entitled Characters, Images, Story Ideas, Dialog, Places/Settings, and so on.

Some writers don't just write down useful and important items in their notebooks, but actually draft most of their pieces in them as well. (These writers usually fill up notebooks very quickly, perhaps one every few months.)

Actually, the term "writer's notebook" can be a bit misleading. You don't have to go out and buy a spiral notebook or three-ring binder. A bound blank book, a legal pad, a set of file folders, a box of loose pages, or a computer disk will all do just as well.

The benefit of an actual notebook is that you can carry it with you wherever you go. As a result, it's always available to make notes in whenever something strikes you—whether it's a conversation you overheard on the subway or a startling image from a dream you had just before dawn.

On the other hand, maybe you don't want the burden of carrying a book around with you all the time. Or perhaps, like me, you want to keep your notebook in your workspace at all times so it can't be lost or misplaced. In such a case, do what I do: simply carry a pen and a blank sheet of paper (or a stack of blank post-it notes) with you. When a thought, observation, or incident strikes you as significant, write it down; then, when you get back to your desk, copy it into your notebook, or place it in the appropriate file folder, or save it on your computer.

YOUR ASSIGNMENT: Think for a few minutes about what sort of writer's notebook will work best for you: a spiral notebook; a blank bound book; a three-ring binder; a legal pad; a set of folders, organized according to dates or topics; computer files; or some other system that I haven't mentioned. Then pick (or design) the one that feels most appropriate.

Exactly how you choose to organize your notebook is entirely up to you, so long as your method is both functional and comfortable. Whatever arrangement you decide on, however, it should be one that lets you add, review, and locate material easily and quickly.

Once you've made your decision, buy whatever items you need. Put your name, addresses, and phone number(s) on your notebook, as protection in case you lose or misplace it. Then divide your notebook into sections and add appropriate section headings.

Now your writer's notebook is ready, and you're ready to begin writing. You'll use your notebook to complete Steps 4, 5, 6, and 7—and to support and inform your writing for many years to come.

When your notebook is full, save it in an easily-accessible place, and start another one. Over the years you may accumulate dozens of notebooks, each of which may prove to be a rich source of material.

STEP 4

Determine and Record
Your Goals

Setting realistic goals can help you to get started writing—and, once you've started, they can help you to *keep on* writing, week after week and month after month, as your skills steadily develop.

Once you reach each goal, you can look back and appreciate how far you have come, how much you have achieved, and how well your efforts have paid off. (And even if you *don't* succeed in reaching a particular goal, it will still have proven useful, because it will have encouraged you to put forth serious and sustained effort.)

Setting reasonable goals isn't always easy. It's tempting to start off with highly ambitious goals—but the more ambitious they are, the easier it is to fall short of them or to grow discouraged. Remember, you're setting writing goals entirely for your own benefit—so set attainable ones. *The most effective goals are those that are tough enough to make you stretch, and maybe even sweat, but not so distant or difficult that you're likely to give up in frustration.*

The best writing goals are specific and concrete—for example, "to complete three short opinion pieces on education" or "to spend two hours a day, four days a week writing essays on education." "To write up my ideas on education," while a perfectly legitimate intention, is too amorphous and unspecific to serve as a useful goal.

Here are some examples of clear, effective, realistic writing goals. (You may wish to adopt one or more of them for your first year as a writer.)

- To write for at least two hours a week, and to see where this takes you.
- To write at least three short stories that you're reasonably happy with.
- To keep a writer's notebook for a minimum of six months, and to use material from that notebook to create at least four finished pieces.
- To write at least one essay every two months, and, after ten months, to submit the three best essays to magazines, newspapers, and/or websites for publication.
- To write for an hour a day, four days a week, and to try your hand at writing poetry, fiction, prose poems, and essays.
- To go through *30 Steps to Becoming a Writer* from beginning to end, completing every one of the 30 steps.

Any goal that you set for your writing should reflect your own efforts rather than the judgments and decisions of others. Having a poem accepted for publication by a literary magazine within a year may sound like a reasonable goal at first—but it's based on the decisions of editors, who can be quirky and capricious. A better goal for your first year as a writer might be to write several poems that you genuinely feel are *worthy of publication* by literary magazines, and to submit those poems to the editors of at least three such magazines. *This* goal is based solely on your own efforts and ability, not on the decisions of others.

But what if you're not an especially goal-oriented person— or if you're not even sure whether writing is something you're going to want to keep doing? Then set the following three goals for yourself:

- To write on a regular basis for six months (or some other length of time).
- After six months, to examine your strengths and weaknesses as a writer and to evaluate what you've written.
- To decide where to go and what to do next with your writing.

A great many writers do their best and most productive work when they follow a regular writing schedule. One of your goals, therefore, may be to stick to a writing schedule of your own design. Other writers, however, respond better to the rhythms of their own psyches than they do to those of the clock. If this description fits you, or if your life is simply too unpredictable to allow you to schedule specific writing times in advance, then set a goal to write for a certain *amount* of time each week, but don't commit yourself to a specific schedule. For example: "I'll write three to five hours each week."

If you're not sure whether you'll do better with or without a formal schedule, try both options. You should discover quickly what works best for you.

YOUR ASSIGNMENT: Get out your writer's notebook, and find a group of three or more blank pages. At the top of these pages, write the following:

Page 1   Why I Want to Write
Page 2   Things That Intrigue Me About Writing
Page 3   My Writing Goals for the Year to Come

Start with page 1. On this page, make a list of all of the reasons why you're interested in writing. Don't censor yourself. It doesn't matter whether a reason is selfish or noble, significant or trivial, realistic or pure fantasy. If it's a genuine reason, write it down. Some examples: "to change the world"; "to become wealthy and famous"; "to amuse myself"; "ego gratification"; "catharsis"; "to convince others of certain ideas and beliefs"; "to create great, lasting art"; "to prove to myself that I can write as well as my sister"; "to play with words"; "to find an enjoyable way to make a living on my own"; "to write my grandparents' life story"; "to get more in touch with my feelings"; "to feel more comfortable writing letters, memos, reports, and other everyday items"; "to impress my parents"; "to earn an extra $15,000 or more per year"; "to see my name in print"; "to have a regular outlet for my fantasies"; "to be able to preserve important memories for my children and grandchildren"; "to have a fun and entertaining hobby." Continue adding to this list until it has at least eight items. (If it has many more, that's fine.)

When you've finished this list, turn to page 2 in your notebook. On this page, write down the things that intrigue or interest you about writing. Again, don't censor yourself. Some examples: "the way words can engender emotions in people"; "prose poems"; "imagery"; "presenting people's thoughts in prose, as an internal monolog"; "creating a vivid sense of place"; "twisting reality to make it more moving and exciting"; "making strange or surreal connections"; "choosing just the right details to make something come alive."

When you've finished this second list, stop for a moment. Don't begin setting your specific writing goals just yet. Instead, look at page 33 of this book. You can either write directly on this page in this book or, if you prefer, photocopy the page, fill it out, and place it inside your writer's notebook.

In the upper left of that page you'll see a list of the many different types of literary forms. (Some of these categories overlap; that's okay.) In the lower left you'll see a smaller list of the most common ways in which people make money from their writing. At the end of each list are a few blank lines, on which you may add other areas of interest. To the right of these lists are three columns, headed *YES, NO,* and *MAYBE.*

Over the next 10 minutes, I'd like you to look at each item on the left, one by one, and ask yourself, "Is this something I'd like to spend time writing or doing?" Answer as honestly as you can by placing a check in the appropriate column. If you're unsure or simply don't know, check the *MAYBE* column.

This checklist isn't meant to be definitive, so don't spend a lot of time on it. Simply make your best judgment for each item, based on how you feel about it right now. (You can always change your responses later.) For now, however, this chart will give you a quick overview of what forms of writing interest you and which ones do not.

After you've filled out the checklist completely, put down your pen or pencil, and spend a few minutes looking over all three of the documents you've created: 1) the list of reasons why you want to write, 2) the list of things that intrigue you about writing, and 3) the checklist of literary forms that interest (and don't interest) you.

Now you're ready for page 3. Using the items in these three lists as raw material, come up with *three to five* specific, concrete, and realistic goals that you hope to reach through your writing *within the next year.* (If you need examples, look back at the goals that appear earlier in this step.)

If you come up with more than five goals, write them all down; then look them over carefully, pick the five that mean the most to you, and cross out the others. (You may want to set some of these other goals later, after you have accumulated more writing experience.)

Don't look beyond the first year right now. If a goal means a lot to you but will require more than a year to reach, write it on a separate page and save it for the future.

Once you've written your list of goals, look them over carefully. Do they genuinely cover the things that are most important to you right now? Given your current level of available time, energy, and interest, are they truly realistic and attainable? Is anything about your goals missing, vague, or less than accurate? Make changes or additions as necessary.

Next, put a date at the top of this third list, so that later on you'll be able to look back and see how far you've come, and how long (or short) a time it took you to get there.

Finally, take this list and post it in the place where you write, in a spot where you will see it every time you sit down to write. Or, if you prefer, tape your list of goals on the outside front cover of your writer's notebook.

LITERARY FORMS	YES	NO	MAYBE
Novels			
Short stories			
Memoir/autobiography			
Poetry			
Prose poems			
Spoken word/performance			
Essays			
Creative non-fiction			
Non-fiction books			
Feature articles			
Reporting			
Reviews			
Stage plays			
Audio plays			
TV scripts			
Film scripts			
Songs			
Librettos			
_____			
_____			

TYPES OF PROFESSIONAL WRITING	YES	NO	MAYBE
Writing for publication and/or production			
Writing for organizations			
Ghostwriting/collaborating			
Editing			
_____			
_____			

From now on, each time you sit down to write, make a point to review the list for a few seconds first.

Now you're done with Step 3—and you've completed your first writing assignment. You've discovered a large number of things that are important to you, and you've written them down. You've succeeded in putting words onto paper in a meaningful way.

As the year goes by, keep track of your progress as you come closer and closer to achieving your goals. And keep in mind that *you're* the one who set those goals—which means that you always have the right to change them.

STEP 5

Note Your Interests, Enthusiasms, and Passions

One of the big questions on your mind may be, "Where do writers get their ideas and themes?"—or, to put it more personally, "Where am I going to get mine?"

The answer is that writers find good material *everywhere:* in their memories, experiences, observations, reading, thinking, fantasizing, and obsessing—and simply in being alive and aware.

Perhaps a more important question might be, "How do writers sort through everything they experience, feel, and imagine, in order to decide what's important and what's not?" In other words, how do writers determine what's meaningful to them? And how can you discover what's meaningful to *you?*

The answer to this last question is that *you already know what's meaningful to you*—you just may not have taken the time to spell things out to yourself.

Something is meaningful to you if it generates strong feelings inside of you, or if it makes you stop and pay attention to it, or if you find yourself spending a lot of time doing it, observing it, or thinking about it. If something excites you, scares you, saddens you, delights you, worries you, comforts you, angers you, thrills you, obsesses you, or deeply satisfies you, then it *must* have meaning for you—even if you can't express exactly what that meaning is.

There are literally thousands of things that hold meaning for you. Some of them—for instance, your family, a warm fire on a winter night, the smell of freshly baked bread, the long illness of a friend—may feel important for reasons you can easily explain and understand. Others—the sight of a jogger straining up a hill, an old stone water tower squatting in front of bare winter trees, the smell of gasoline, the sway of a moving subway car—might not be so easy to explain.

As you observe your own life—your own thoughts, actions, and reactions—you'll find that a great many things evoke strong feelings in you. These items are your own natural material, the things for you to use in your writing.

The best way to write well is to write about the things you care about—the things you love, like, hate, fear, worry about, obsess over, yearn for, avoid, can't accept, can't comprehend, or can't come to terms with. The more you work with these things, the more likely you are to move your readers.

You don't have to know how or why something is meaningful to you in order to use it in your writing. Good writing doesn't have to analyze or explain things (though there's nothing inherently wrong with analysis or explanation). However, good writing *does* move and convince readers—by making them care about the same things you care about.

YOUR ASSIGNMENT: Get out your writer's notebook and turn to a blank page. Make sure that several more blank pages follow.

Sit quietly and comfortably for two or three minutes with your notebook open in front of you and a pen or pencil beside it. For those few minutes, don't think or do anything in particular.

Then, slowly, pick up the pen or pencil and begin making a list of those things, people, ideas, sensations, images, events, and actions that move you or somehow have meaning for you. As each item occurs to you, write it down.

Keep your descriptions simple; each item should be no longer than ten or twelve words (e.g., "the night we spent at the Hagens' and ate midnight popovers" or "an old woman sledding, laughing with delight"). Don't write whole sentences or paragraphs, or elaborate descriptions—you can always write these later if you like. Often one or two words (e.g., "rabbit fur," "math anxiety," or "infidelity") is sufficient.

Be as specific as possible. "The way a mother smiles at her child" is fine, but "The way Maria smiled at Rose as she fed the ducks at Lake Nokomis" is better still, because it refers to a specific memory. "Coney Island" is good, but "the smell of electricity, cooking oil, and sugar at Coney Island" is stronger and sharper.

You may find that one item on your list generates half a dozen others. Thus "Coney Island" might prompt you to write down a series of things—"Louisa grabbing the brass ring and falling off the carousel," "kissing Clark on the beach," "mating sand crabs," "my first Nathan's hot dog," "the Parachute Jump," and "getting lost at night at age seven and taking the subway home." Another example: "Justice" might lead to "Thurgood Marshall in the 1960s," "getting punished for what Mark did to Julie," "Jefferson's slaves," "the signs outside Sandstone Prison," "ethics vs. needs," and "Karla's arrest and trial."

Don't censor yourself. No one is going to read your list except you (unless, of course, you invite them to). Don't be afraid to record your obsessions, your irrational fears, your sexual fantasies, or any disturbing images that may appear. Whatever comes, let it come; you may be able to use it in your writing, either as is or altered. In fact, some of those things that disturb or frighten you may result in some of your most gripping and powerful writing, precisely *because* they disturb or frighten you. (Many writers—Edgar Allan Poe, for example—created some of their very best work by drawing on their fantasies and fears.) Of course, if you choose later not to work with any of the items that disturb you, that's fine. But write them down for the moment, so that you don't lose or forget them.

If you're having trouble getting started, begin your list with these four items, which just about everyone cares about:
• Sex • Sleep • Food • Death

See if you can list some specific images, events, or concerns for each of the four. Once you've done that, continue adding new items of your own.

Go as fast or as slowly as you need to. If you have to search your mind and heart carefully, that's fine. If the items come pouring out on their own, that's fine, too.

Continue compiling this list, filling up as many pages as you need to, until you feel yourself naturally beginning to wind down. Keep going for 2-3 minutes more, then stop.

Most people finish up after 15-30 minutes; but if you're still going strong at the end of half an hour, keep writing for as long as the words keep flowing—but for no more than an hour in all.

When you've finished, look over your list—which will probably run several pages—from beginning to end. It will almost certainly include a diverse range of subjects and emotions. Some of the items on the list will be people, things, and events that have stuck with you for years; other items may appear to have come completely out of the blue. Some may be things you have forgotten for years and suddenly remembered again. All of these items, however, may eventually prove useful to your writing.

If additional ideas or images come to you as you read your list—and they probably will—write these down as well.

༽

Now put your list away for a while—at least a day, and ideally a week or two. Then come back to your favorite writing spot, prepare yourself with plenty of blank pages, and get ready to repeat the process—but this time with a difference.

As before, relax and get comfortable for a couple of minutes. This time, however, instead of making a deliberate, conscious list, *don't* try to make any list at all. Simply close your eyes and follow your breath for about ten minutes. Observe it as it goes into your body, pauses briefly, then is exhaled back out.

If your mind wanders during this process—and it probably will—gently bring it back to your breathing again. Just breathe, watch your breath, and gently bring your attention back as necessary.

After ten minutes have passed, slowly pick up your pen or pencil and turn your attention to the blank pages in front of you. This time, though, instead of consciously searching your memory and heart for the things that move you, *don't search for anything at all*. Instead, simply let your mind wander wherever it pleases. Don't try to direct or control it.

Things will pop into your consciousness, stay there for a time, and then disappear again, to be replaced by other thoughts and images. Some will be mundane, others fraught with meaning. Some will surprise or shock you; others will please or excite or delight you. Whenever something moving or meaningful appears, write it down.

Continue this process for half an hour, then stop.

Look through your second list carefully, adding any new items that may come to mind as you review it. Then compare it to the more deliberate list you created earlier. Which list is longer? Which contains the items that you find the most moving and meaningful? Which list intrigues or inspires you more?

If the first list has the most or best material, then you probably work best by deliberately searching among your concerns, ideas, images, and memories; if your second list seems stronger, then you probably work better intuitively, using a less deliberate process of letting your mind wander at will.

Save both of your lists indefinitely. They will serve as source material for your writing for months or years to come.

In the future, whenever you're unsure what to write next—or when you're stuck for the right line, image, idea, character, event, element, or plot twist—simply look over your lists again. Chances are good that you'll find what you need somewhere on them.

More important, add to either or both lists on a regular basis. You can two this in two different ways. First, add important ideas, events, images, and memories whenever they spontaneously occur to you. Second, you can spend 15-30 minutes a week generating more material for either list—or for both. You can do this week after week, year after year if you like.

These two processes will provide you with never-ending sources of ideas and images to work from—a huge vein of material to mine whenever you like.

∞

Now look back at what you've accomplished in this step. You've answered *for yourself* the question, "Where do I get material for my writing?" Furthermore, you've discovered a source of material—your own memories, feelings, images, concerns, and ideas—that will constantly replenish itself year after year.

And now for the best news of all: there are still two other sources of material for your writing that you've not yet explored, and each one is rich with detail and meaning. In Steps 6 and 7 I'll introduce you to them, and you'll discover how to use them both to deepen and strengthen your writing.

STEP 6

Record Your Observations

You've now learned two different ways to reach into your heart, your mind, and your memories for material that moves and affects you. In this step, you'll explore a different, but equally inexhaustible, source of material: your day-by-day experience.

Each of us, no matter who we are, can draw from this rich and profound source. What we live through, encounter, and observe can continually provide us with useful insights, ideas, and images. This is as true for the housewife who has never left rural Indiana as it is for the internationally-famous actress who has traveled the world. We need only learn how to direct our full attention to each moment as we live it.

While some of us have a wider variety of experiences than others, all of us share the same fundamental human feelings, problems, and concerns. We all have desires, dreams, needs, fears, disappointments, and worries. We have all experienced joy, loss, loneliness, shock, delight, despair, and a multitude of other feelings. In this sense, your life is fundamentally no different from the lives of all other human beings on the planet; only the external particulars differ. This is why a factory worker in Denver can enjoy reading a story about a fisherman from Taiwan, a poem about a philosopher from Venice, a play about a Russian thief, or an essay about Peruvian farmers. It is also why others can appreciate and empathize with *your* experience, regardless of how expansive or limited it may be.

Often we fail to appreciate just how large, profound, and vivid our own lives can be. Instead of fully engaging with each moment as it appears before us, we separate ourselves from it and hold parts of ourselves back. Our habit is to focus only a small part of our attention on what's happening around us— just enough to get the gist of things and categorize them ("a cloudy sky," "a huge oak desk," "an angry, tired clerk"). The rest of our attention gets set aside, to think, evaluate, or be concerned with other things. We don't participate in the fullness of the moment.

Yet if we were to truly focus our attention on any one person, object, or event—even for a few seconds—we would frequently find it rich with detail, significance, and meaning. We would discover that much of our everyday existence is, in fact, vivid, rich, abundant, and, quite often, genuinely astonishing.

If you are alert and observant, every moment of your life can provide you with material for your writing. Your task is to pick those incidents, observations, and ideas that are most significant and most worth relating to others.

"But how will I know what in my day-to-day experience is significant and what's not?" I hear you ask.

You'll know in the same way that you knew in Step 5 what was meaningful for you. If something moves you in some way— if it delights you, disturbs you, shocks you, angers you, pleases you, confuses you, haunts you, panics you, or simply sticks with you over time—then it has real significance for you, and is worth writing about.

And what should you do when you experience a meaningful incident, observation, image, dialog, or thought? Write it down in your notebook.

YOUR ASSIGNMENTS: Completing this step involves four brief but very different tasks.

1. Find a building you've never been inside of before. This can be an office building, a warehouse, an unusual home, an air-

craft hangar, a hotel, an abandoned factory—any building that intrigues you. Find a room in this building where you can be completely alone for fifteen minutes.

Enter the room and, if possible, close the door behind you. Then scan the entire room slowly and carefully, including the ceiling and floor. Take note of the colors, textures, designs, and angles. Notice the different materials used to construct the walls, the floor, the windows, and the ceiling. Observe any details that might not be visible at first—sprinkler heads, moldings, graffiti, broken window latches, chipped paint, and so on. Then take a walk around the room, observing it from different angles. Look for new details with each step.

As you walk, run your hand along various surfaces, noting how they feel, including their textures, temperatures, and angles. Also pay attention to how the floor feels beneath your feet.

When you've walked completely around the room, stop and stand still. For a minute or two, listen to all of the sounds in the room—e.g., the whoosh of air blowing in through heating vents, the dull throb of machinery, the creak of old beams in the wind, the rattle of a loose window, voices drifting in from outside, or the sound of your own breathing.

Now focus your attention on the air in the room. Is it dry or moist, warm or cool? Does it smell fresh, musty, salty, greasy, disinfected? Are other smells wafting in from outside?

Next, carefully examine some of the objects in the room. Pick the three to six that seem most interesting to you. One by one, pick them up or run your hands over them. Turn then over—or kneel down—and examine them from unusual angles. Hold them against your cheek or elbow, or the back of your knee. Put your nose up against each of them and inhale deeply.

Finally, look at the entire room from two or three unusual perspectives. Lie down on the floor—first on your back, then on your stomach; stand on a desk or table and look down; crawl inside a closet or cabinet or secluded corner and peer out. Spend two to three minutes observing the room from each of these vantage points. Then leave the room.

Once you're outside, review some of the most striking or unusual things you noticed about the room. What surprised you? What did you find out that you hadn't known or thought about before? What about the room affected or intrigued you? Write down these items in your notebook.

In doing this first assignment, you've taught yourself to carefully observe, to look for details that might not be immediately apparent, and to view the same setting, object, or event from a variety of angles. You can use this technique, which I call close observation, anywhere and at any time you choose. You can use it over and over in the future—not just for settings and places, but for objects, people, concepts, actions, incidents, and events.

This technique will often yield insights, connections, and meanings that you might ordinarily overlook. The more you practice close observation, the easier it will get, the better you will get at it, and the more natural it will become for you.

In the future, whenever something catches your attention or strikes you as important, intriguing, or worth noticing, stop what you're doing for a short time and switch into this close observation mode. For a minute or two—or, if your time is very limited, for a few attentive seconds—focus your full, one-pointed attention on that object, person, setting, or event. Take note of all the details, nuances, and key images. In particular, note any surprises—things that seem ironic or unexpected or out of place.

Then, as soon as possible, write down what you observed that feels significant or important. Sometimes this may mean writing down all of your observations, item by item and detail by detail. At other times, it may be enough to jot down only a few key words, such as "Martina's attic," if these will be enough to bring a complete, detailed memory vividly to life for you.

If you don't have time to write down all of your close observations immediately, jot down the key items as notes; then, as soon as possible—but certainly within 24 hours—come back to your notebook, reread your notes, and write out everything in as much detail as necessary.

With practice, you'll soon be able to engage in close observation at a moment's notice, whenever something moves or intrigues you.

2. Use the technique of close observation once again—but, this time, instead of going to a place you've never been, do something you've never done, something vastly outside your usual routine. Take a balloon ride. Spend an evening in a bikers' bar. Attend a prayer service at a mosque, or a Mormon temple, or a Quaker meeting house. Go to a Vietnamese karaoke nightclub. Take a guided tour of something you'd never normally visit—a sewage treatment plant, a canning factory, or an ore boat. The activity can be something you've always wanted to do, or it can be something you've always been a bit afraid of (but don't put yourself in any real danger). Other people should be part of the activity, but don't do it with someone you know—go it alone, so that you are fully immersed in the experience.

3. Go to some public place where you feel comfortable—a park, a coffee shop, a hotel lobby—at a time when there are likely to be lots of people around. Bring your notebook and a couple of pens or pencils with you. Find a spot near the center of the action, get comfortable, and open your notebook on your lap.

For the next 45 to 60 minutes, deliberately eavesdrop on the conversations of the people near you, including those of the people who walk past. Focus your attention not only on what each person says, but on the inflections, accents, and emotions in their voices as well. Note how each person is dressed, how they hold themselves, how they gesture, how they smell, and so on. Write down anything that intrigues, amuses, moves, or inspires you.

Be discreet in all your observations, of course. Don't give people any clues that you're listening in; in fact, to preserve your anonymity and safety, it's best to look in a different direction most of the time.

Later, when you get back to your desk, look over what you've written down. If anything in your notes leads to more ideas, images, or connections, write these down as well.

Once you've done this, you've learned yet another useful, important, and deceptively-simple technique for finding and developing material for your writing. You've learned how to draw from others' experience as well as your own.

You've done something else as well. By actively listening to what others have to say and letting it spark ideas, images, and connections of your own, you've combined your experience with theirs. You can use this technique of drawing fresh material from other people's lives any time you wish.

4. Put your notebook and a couple of pens or pencils next to your bed before you go to sleep. The next morning, as soon as you awaken, open the notebook and spend ten minutes reviewing your dreams from the night before, as well as any ideas and insights you may have had while falling asleep or waking up. Write down anything that seems significant or meaningful. (If you wake up in the middle of the night, feel free to do the same things then, especially if images from a vivid dream remain with you.)

Take your notebook with you throughout the day, jotting down notes in it whenever something catches your attention or moves you.

Then, toward the end of your day—sometime between supper and sleep—take about twenty minutes to review and reflect on the events of the day. Write down whatever insights, ideas, and observations come to you.

This simple practice of making regular notes and doing a daily review of your experience can result in a wealth of rich and important material. Try it for three or four days in a row; then use it again as often as you wish. If you like, make it a part of your regular daily activities.

You've accomplished a great deal in Step 6. You've learned several techniques for observing the world more closely, for recording those observations, and for turning close observation into a habit. Most important of all, you've gotten some hands-on experience in using your daily life as a source of material for your writing.

Now you're ready to begin tying some of this material together.

STEP 7

Put Your Thoughts and Ideas on Paper

So far you've discovered two abundant and easily-accessible sources of material for your writing: your past—including your memories, thoughts, and feelings—and your present—your current experiences and observations. In this step you'll explore a third wellspring of material: your ability to make connections, associations, and logical and intuitive leaps. You'll create something new out of the material you've accumulated from other sources.

Each of us is constantly analyzing, synthesizing, and evaluating the information that flows into our minds and hearts. We do this in order to create an internal picture of the universe in which we live. Each of us tries to form as accurate a picture as possible; nevertheless, each person's internal picture will always be unique.

This process takes place both consciously and subconsciously. Your conscious mind weighs evidence, sifts through information, and comes to conclusions; your subconscious speaks to you through feelings, hunches, dreams, and intuition. Both parts of this process, however, involve asking yourself these central questions: what is most important, meaningful, or intriguing to me? What interests me, fascinates me, or moves me?

The more closely you pay attention to these questions, the more vivid and telling your writing is likely to be, the more likely it is to move and convince others, and the more satisfaction and pleasure you are likely to gain from creating it. In short, the more you remain true to your own cares, concerns, and impulses, the more your readers will be able to empathize with you, understand you, and appreciate what you have to say.

YOUR ASSIGNMENTS: This step involves three brief tasks:

1. Take out your writer's notebook, a pen or pencil, and several blank sheets of paper. These should be loose pages, so that you don't have to keep flipping back and forth in your notebook.

Slowly and carefully, look over everything you wrote as you completed the assignments in Steps 4, 5, and 6. Also look at any additional notes you may have made during the same period. As you examine and consider all of these notes, do several things:

First, look for any ideas, images, themes, people, locations, or even specific words that appear repeatedly. For instance, you may find that *scenes* from your childhood, or from past winters, or from Germany, or from baseball games, occur often. Maybe similar *settings* —such as streets, roads, alleys, and paths—appear frequently. Or perhaps food, or jazz, or solitude, or danger, or fear of aging appears as a recurrent *theme.*

The same *person or people* —your grandmother, for instance, or teachers, or public officials—may appear over and over. Maybe there is a common *viewpoint* —the outsider looking in, or the seeker hoping to make sense of things, or the discontented critic hoping to change things for the better. Or perhaps what surfaces is a particular kind of *relationship:* the relationship of individuals to government, or of emotional expression to spiritual development, or of psychology to education, or of adolescence to middle age. Or maybe you see a unity of certain kinds of *images*: images of poverty, or of light, or of sudden change, or of aimless movement, or of the large enveloping the small. Whatever connections and patterns emerge, write them down on the loose sheets of paper.

But don't simply note those connections; explore on those sheets of paper what these connections mean to you, and write down any further thoughts, images, or incidents that these associations lead you to. Don't hold yourself back or censor yourself;

write it all down, using as many words and pages as you need to. If one thing leads to another, and then to another, and then to yet another, that's wonderful. If, by the time you're done, you've completed a draft (or a substantial portion of a draft) of a story, poem, or essay, that's better still.

As you're doing all this, observe your own mental and emotional reactions. What things do you respond to most strongly or enthusiastically—or most anxiously or fearfully? Mark each of these items in some way—by underlining it, or circling it, or placing a star before it. *Each of these items can become the basis for a poem, story, essay, or other piece of writing.*

2. Now that you've become familiar not only with the things that you care about, but with some of the relationships among them, you're ready to take the process a step further.

Look again at all the things you've written on the loose sheets of paper, as well as at any highlighted (underlined, starred, etc.) items on those sheets or in your notebook. (If you've got lots of different items to choose from, feel free to limit yourself to the five or six that most attract you.) For each of these items, ask yourself the following questions:

- What most interests, intrigues, fascinates, or moves me about this?
- What would I most like to do with it?
- What do I most want to say about it?
- What would I most like to see happen with it or to it?
- What would I most like to read about it, or in relation to it?

For each item you've chosen, take a separate loose page and write down your answers to all of these questions. Again, don't limit or censor yourself, or force yourself to stick to what may seem reasonable, appropriate, or socially acceptable.

As you answer these questions, all sorts of concepts, images, and events—perhaps even entire paragraphs, stanzas, or plots—may pop into your mind. If so, great. Write them down.

Many of these may appear to come out of nowhere. Some will make immediate sense, but others may at first seem inappropriate or irrelevant. *Write them all down anyway.* Often your subconscious will make an intuitive leap that doesn't consciously seem to fit—but as you write further, the wisdom of this seemingly-illogical connection (or, at least, a way to make the connection work) will eventually reveal itself to you.

3. Look at the loose pages you've filled in response to the second assignment above. Each page can serve as a set of working notes for a complete piece of writing. Each page can also serve as a springboard for getting started.

Your final assignment is to look over these pages carefully, then pick one to work with. (You can always work with any or all of the others later.) This page will form the basis for your first complete piece of writing, which you'll be writing from start to finish in Steps 9-21.

In this step you've learned to work with your memories and experience—and to build on them. You've also taught yourself to note significant relationships in your material, as well as to create new ones. You can repeat this process any time you please to discover connections, make associations, reach conclusions, or begin creating a new piece of writing.

STEP 8

Forget the "Have-To's"

Throughout our lives, each of us has been taught a variety of shoulds, musts, and have-to's. While some of these make a great deal of sense ("stop on red, go on green"), others are questionable ("eat a hearty breakfast every morning"), and still others are downright nonsense ("always finish one project before starting another").

Some of the shoulds that we learned over the years involve writing. We learned them from English teachers, from books about writing, from editors, from other writers, and from a variety of other sources.

When it comes to the conventions of grammar, spelling, punctuation, and sentence structure, many of these shoulds and musts make sense. So do the standards for preparing and submitting manuscripts to editors (which I'll discuss in detail in Steps 26 and 28). These conventions and standards, while arbitrary, serve to make reading, writing, and editing easier for everyone.

But a great many of the supposed shoulds, musts, and have-to's that relate to writing are actually quite useless. Often they reflect nothing more than the biases, preferences, or ignorance of the people who advocate them. Sometimes they're outmoded or obsolete, yet they've been passed on, unquestioned, from generation to generation. In other cases, they may be useful for some people, but useless or even counterproductive for others. (For instance, some writers need to adhere to a regular schedule or they can't write at all, while others find that a schedule gets in the way of their inspiration and creativity.)

The best way to deal with these shoulds is to get them out

into the open, acknowledge them as useless or harmful, and then simply ignore or forget them.

What follows is a list of the most common shoulds, musts, and have-to's that many of us have been taught about writing. Each of these is either useless, irrelevant, or just plain incorrect:

- You should work on only one piece of writing at a time.
- You must write every day, or for a minimum amount of time every day.
- You must write a certain number of words or pages each day.
- If you're serious about writing, you must make it your top priority at all times.
- You must write according to a regular schedule.
- You should have a separate room to do your writing in.
- A writer must be unhappy, or lonely, or cynical, or 100% serious, or neurotic, or a little crazy, or downright nuts.
- If you wish to be published, you must do whatever editors ask.
- You must be completely free from all distractions and interruptions in order to write well.
- You should stubbornly resist any editor's attempts to change your work.
- You must bare your soul in your writing, and/or write about the most personal and intimate things in your life.
- You must dress and act in a certain way, and/or associate with certain people, in order to be a successful writer.
- In order to be published, you have to know (and/or kiss up to) the right people.
- You should always write an outline before you begin your first draft.
- You must write your title first.
- You must write the various sections of your piece in the same sequence in which they will be read.
- You must know how your piece will end before you begin writing it.

- You must always write "he or she," "him or her," or "his or her" when referring to hypothetical people.
- You should always put the most exciting or important part of your piece at the very beginning, so that it will grab your readers.
- You must always begin each piece with something shocking or exciting, or else you risk losing your reader.
- You must always write a minimum of two (or three, or four, or five) drafts. First drafts will never be any good.
- You must keep each of your manuscripts circulating among editors until it is accepted for publication.
- If a manuscript is rejected, you must get it back out to another editor within 24 hours.
- To protect yourself against literary theft, you must register everything you write with the government copyright office, and/or you must mail yourself a copy of each piece as soon as it's completed.
- You must type your social security number, a proper copyright notice (e.g., Copyright 2004 by Scott Edelstein), and the rights you wish to sell on the first page of each of your manuscripts.

The only sane response to any of these pronouncements is a loud and emphatic, **"NOT SO!"** None of them is universally true. Some may be useful or true for some writers, or under certain circumstances. Some may be helpful as generalities, but are not absolutes. Many—the last seven, for example—are pure baloney through and through.

In addition to the shoulds, writers also face a barrage of equally worthless shouldn'ts. Here are the most common examples:

- Never write about yourself.
- Never write in the first person, or use the words "I," "me," or "my."
- Never use curse words, slang, or colloquialisms.
- Never use italics.

- Never use exclamation points.
- Never use foreign words.
- Never start a sentence with "and," "but," "anyway," "however," "nevertheless," "therefore," or "I."
- Never use incomplete sentences.
- Never stray from correct grammar and usage for any reason.
- Never write in dialect; always use standard English.
- Never send something you've written to more than one editor at once.
- Never submit photocopied manuscripts to editors.
- Never rewrite, except to editorial order.

I repeat: all of these are worthless at best, harmful at worst. Ignore them all.

There is yet another type of nonsense that we writers often face: strange beliefs about what makes a writer. It's common for people—usually literature professors, editors, or writers with overblown egos—to try to tell us who is a writer and who isn't. These folks like to proclaim that no one can legitimately call themselves a writer (or, at least, a real writer) unless they have done one of the following:

- Written (or published) at least two (or three, or ten, or twenty) books.
- Had at least two (or five, or fifty) pieces published.
- Been writing for at least two (or five, or fifteen) years.
- Written at least a million words.
- Been writing full-time, or for a certain minimum number of hours per week, for a year (or five, or ten).
- Worked a variety of jobs, or traveled throughout much of the world, or had plenty of experience with the "real world."
- Read and studied the great works of western (or world) literature.
- Received a Master of Fine Arts (MFA) degree in writing.
- Suffered (or suffered prodigiously).
- Had their work rejected at least 100 (or 500, or 1000) times.

All of these pronouncements are nothing less than absurd.

If someone says that you must have published at least five books in order to be a writer, the odds are very good that this person has published at least five books. And if someone believes that you need to have completed an MFA degree in order to be a real writer, I'll bet you dollars to gumballs that they have an MFA diploma hanging on their wall.

I've never quite understood why certain people feel a need to define for the rest of the world who is a writer and who isn't. Do you know anyone who spends their time explaining to the world that only certain people deserve to be called real plumbers? ("Unless you've fixed at least 250 leaky toilets . . .")

It ought to be obvious—at least, it's obvious to me—that anyone who writes is a writer, just as anyone who rides a bicycle is a bicyclist, and anyone who golfs is a golfer. Whether you're an experienced writer, or a professional writer (i.e., someone who makes all or part of their living through their writing), or even a talented writer are different questions, of course.

YOUR ASSIGNMENT: This one's easy.

First, photocopy the three lists that appear in this chapter—the shoulds, the shouldnt's, and the aren'ts. Then post these lists in a fairly prominent place; hang them on a wall or bulletin board in the place where you write, or tape them inside your notebook. At the top of each page, write in large letters, "Bad Advice—Ignore." Or, if you prefer, draw a circle with a diagonal line through it (the visual equivalent of "NOT!") on each page.

Second, know these items for what they are: baloney. Because you may have learned some of them as absolutes when you were younger, however, you may need to unlearn them. That's why you've posted the lists in a prominent spot: so that you'll see them regularly and be able to remind yourself that you don't have to follow them or believe in them.

Third, ignore these statements when you hear other people declare them, when you read them in books, or when they pop up in your own mind as you write. And some of them *will* pop up now and then, out of sheer habit. When they arise, threatening to redirect you or get in your way, simply stop for a moment. Check to be sure what you're thinking is on one of the three lists. Once you've found it, reassure yourself that it's as silly and useless as you thought, and mentally toss that pompous prescription over your shoulder. Then get back to the business of writing.

By now you've bought all the supplies you need. You've set up your workplace, started your writer's notebook, discovered several inexhaustible sources of material for your writing, and learned how to access each of those sources at will. You've trained yourself to observe more fully, to focus on the things that matter to you, and to put together ideas and images in a meaningful way. And you've learned to ignore the so-called rules that get in your way.

With these skills and experiences under your belt, you're ready to start writing a story, poem, essay or other piece of creative writing from start to finish.

PART 2

Getting Your Words Out

STEP 9

Pick a Starting Point

Two of the most common—and most anxiety-producing— questions that beginning writers ask themselves are, 1) "Where do I begin?" and 2) "How do I get started?"

The answer to the first question is quite simple: You can begin anywhere you like. There are no rules, requirements, or absolutes.

Writing isn't like performing a piece of music. If you're performing a piano concerto, you've got to play all of the notes and chords in the proper sequence. But if you're writing an essay, poem, or story, nobody is going to see what you've written until you're ready to show it to them. This means that you don't have to write your piece in the order in which it is to be read. You can always arrange and rearrange the parts later.

If you're writing a short story, for example, you might write the closing paragraph first, then the rest of the final scene, then the first two scenes, and then, as your intuition and desires direct you, the scenes in between.

In some cases, you might not even know how to order your scenes until you've written most or all of them. Many writers, in fact, begin by writing the scenes that most intrigue or excite them, without regard for where they will appear in the finished piece. Only later do they concern themselves with fitting them together.

Other writers like to write the easiest parts of a piece first, then work on the more difficult sections. This enables them to build up momentum, so that they can keep writing when the going gets tough.

Your freedom to begin anywhere also refers to the sequence of events, images, or ideas that appear in your piece. Suppose, for example, that you decide to write a personal essay chronicling your eight years as a Newfoundland fisherman. You could begin by recounting the day you first stepped onto a fishing boat as a teenager. Or you could begin earlier, with the fascination you felt for the sea as a child—or earlier still, at age four, when you first wondered where the fish on your dinner plate came from.

Or you could, if you preferred, begin your essay in the present and look back on your years as a fisherman from your current perspective. Or you might begin with your very last day as a fisherman, comparing that day to other working days two, five, and eight years earlier.

Beginning your piece anywhere you choose also applies to the specific material that you work with. You might, for example, decide to start by working with a *character* —say, your great aunt. You could begin by recounting your earliest recollection of her, or by recreating a discussion the two of you had a few weeks ago, or by using her voice and viewpoint to describe life in France under the Nazi occupation during World War II.

You could also begin writing your piece with a specific *incident, scene,* or *event* —either real or imaginary—such as the rescue of two half-drowned children from a flooded basement, the final inning of the 1960 World Series, the landing of the first manned spacecraft on Mars, or the reunion of elderly twin brothers after spending forty years apart.

Another good place to begin is with a strong *image,* which is a set of sensory impressions. (An image can involve any of the five senses, and often combines two or three different ones.) Some examples: a pair of deer dashing across a highway; the hail rattling against a rusting bulldozer; hot air balloons rising above fields of ripening corn; a Tibetan family sitting, still and silent, in meditation. (William Faulkner's novel *The Sound and the Fury* grew out of a single image that Faulkner had of a small child climbing a tree in her underwear. Ursula K. LeGuin's novel *The Left Hand of Darkness* developed from a mental picture she had of two people pulling a sled together through a snow-covered arctic landscape.)

Many successful pieces begin with a *setting,* which is an image that creates a strong sense of place. Examples of settings include: a marsh with morning steam rising from it; the afternoon rush-hour traffic jam on the George Washington Bridge; an abandoned cabin overgrown with vines; the glitzy lounge of a cruise ship, heavy with chandeliers and chrome.

It's also possible to begin building your piece around a *theme* or *concept.* Examples here might include stopping the growth of inner-city gangs; why America should have a democratically-elected king and queen; how activists on both side of the abortion debate believe they are protecting our civilization from barbarism; or why El Paso is a far more American city than Washington, D.C.

Many writers have used a single strong line, statement, or *quote* as their entryway into a piece. Some examples: "We always had to look good in airports"; "The new moon hangs in the old moon's shadow"; "I smell the coming rain"; "Sometimes I think the whole world is on back order"; "What Velveeta is to cheese, Elizabeth was to nursing." Often—but not necessarily—these become the first or last lines of successful pieces.

You can also, if you wish, begin by outlining a specific *plot,* or sequence of events. Despite what you may have been taught in high school or college, however, you don't have to prepare an outline in order to get started. It's entirely optional—and, for many writers, counterproductive. (I'll discuss outlines, and some useful variations and alternatives, in Step 16).

In fact, you don't have to know how or where your finished piece will begin in order to start writing. For that matter, you don't have to know how it will end, or where it will go, or even what it will ultimately say, do, or focus on. Indeed, in many cases it is only *after* you have started writing a piece that you will discover what you have to say in it. Writing often comes first, and content, structure, and focus second.

Mysterious? Yes. Unusual? Not at all.

This step began with two questions: "Where do I begin?" and "How do I get started?" The answer to the second question is even simpler than the answer to the first: you get started by writing, by putting words on paper or a computer screen. This involves no magic, no special tricks, and no complicated training. You just do it, one word, phrase, or line at a time.

YOUR ASSIGNMENT: Look over all your notes for the first piece you have chosen to write. Based on these notes, pick a basic form or *genre* to work with—e.g., fiction, nonfiction, poetry, prose poetry (poetry written in paragraphs rather than stanzas), etc. (See Step 4 for a complete list of genres and forms.)

Next, pick a specific place to start. This might be a scene, an event, an image, a character, a certain viewpoint, a setting, a concept, a quote, a theme, an intriguing line or statement, or anything else that deeply affects you, or that feels like it can open up into much more.

Now find a series of blank pages in your notebook and write. If it's only one line or sentence, that's fine; if it's a whole scene or stanza, that's even better.

When you've finished writing this beginning, keep on writing. Continue until you reach a natural stopping place. Then take a break and turn to Step 10.

STEP 10

Write a First Draft

Each version of a piece of writing is called a *draft*. A *first draft* is your initial attempt at writing your piece more or less from beginning to end.

Your first draft may bear only a passing resemblance to the final draft you'll eventually write. Much of your first draft may be awkward, sketchy, and unfocused—but that's quite common. A first draft isn't supposed to be polished or flawless; it's just supposed to give you something of substance to work with.

Keep two things in mind when writing a first draft:

1) Your guiding principles at all times should be the questions, "What moves, intrigues, or fascinates *me*?" and "What do I want to say, do, see, or have happen in this piece?"

2) Your primary focus should be on getting the words onto the page (or the computer screen). Keep the flow and momentum going.

Don't worry about getting things exactly right. Smoothness, clarity, and detail will come later, with subsequent drafts, revision, and/or editing. If you can't come up with quite the right word, phrase, image, or connection that you want, spend a *brief* amount of time—a minute at most—searching for it. If the right words don't come, don't get bogged down looking for them. Make a note to yourself in the appropriate spot (e.g., "stronger image of decay here," "make dialog angrier," etc.), or simply leave a blank space. Then move on to the next sentence or line. After your first draft is complete, you can come back, focus your full attention on the difficult passage, and work with it until it sounds and feels right.

It can be tempting to edit, censor, or critique your words as they flow out of you. *Resist this temptation and keep writing.* Don't distract yourself from your task of creating a complete (if imperfect) version of your piece.

At times what you write may strike you as vague, awkward, confusing, shocking, silly, inappropriate, or just plain wrong. That's OK; let it be that way. Remind yourself that you'll have plenty of opportunity to work on it later. Just keep writing.

As your piece develops, unexpected words, phrases, images, and ideas may come to you. Some of these may work in strange or surprising ways. If they sound or feel right, by all means use them. If you're not sure about them, however, jot them down briefly and continue in the direction you've been going. You may find a use for them later on. They may also provide a solution if you find yourself getting lost or stuck as you write further.

Sometimes, despite your plans and intentions, your piece may start to move in a new and unexpected direction, seemingly of its own accord. This is both common and natural: pieces of writing often change and evolve as they're being created. Keep in mind that you're not obliged to stick to your original plan or structure; if a new focus, theme, viewpoint, or direction emerges, feel free to explore it.

Trust your hunches and intuition. If something feels right, it's probably worth trying. If it doesn't take you anywhere worthwhile, or if the piece starts to change into something you don't want it to become, you can always return to your original plan.

There may also be times when you simply don't know what to do or where to go next. You may find yourself at a crossroads, with two or more different directions or options to choose from—each one equally tempting. Or you might feel lost or stuck, with no idea at all what your next step should be. In either of these cases, simply ask yourself once again, "What do I most want to see, do, say, or have happen here? What will most move, excite, or interest me?" Your answer to these questions should provide you with a direction.

If it doesn't, however, stop writing for the moment. Often it helps to take your cues from what you've already written—so go back and reread all the notes you've written on the piece, as well as what you've written in your first draft so far. The follow whatever ideas, hunches, or gut reactions come to you.

If this doesn't get you going again, open up your writer's notebook and scan its pages. Chances are excellent that something you've recorded in it will provide the right creative spark.

If, despite all your efforts, you still find yourself stuck, don't despair. Try one or more of the following:

• Rewrite or retype your last page, then keep going.
• Write something else for a while—preferably something that comes easily to you, such as a letter or a notebook entry.
• Change how, when, or where you write. Sometimes a change in your scenery, schedule, or work habits can give you a new perspective.
• Stop writing, but don't leave your workspace. Sit quietly for several minutes, deliberately *not* thinking about your piece and *not* trying to solve your problem. Follow your breath in and out of your body, and let your mind wander. For the next half hour, observe what bubbles up naturally into your consciousness; if something seems promising, write it down.
• Give yourself a time out, and take your mind *off* the subject for a while. Take a walk, see a movie, eat lunch, or take a nap. Then, refreshed, return to your piece.
• Promise yourself a reward of something you like very much once you've solved your problem. Be sure to give yourself this reward once you've found a solution or direction.
• Brainstorm with one or more other people about new ideas, directions, and approaches for the piece.

- If you work well under pressure, set a reasonable deadline for getting unstuck—say, 45 or 60 minutes from now. Then stick to it.
- If necessary, put the piece aside for a day or two. Give your conscious mind a rest and your subconscious a chance to work on the problem.

Unless you plan to write a very short piece, don't expect to write a full first draft in a single sitting. You may need several writing sessions—perhaps more than several—to produce a complete draft.

In each writing session, work until you feel your time, energy, inspiration, or enthusiasm beginning to run low. Then keep going a little longer, until you come to a natural stopping place. When you reach this point, quit writing for the moment. Spend the next five to ten minutes making notes on where the piece might go next and what it might do and include. Finish up your writing session by rereading aloud everything that you've done on your piece so far.

What if, after working on your piece for some time, you realize that you've lost interest in it? Put that piece aside for now (but *don't* throw it away) and choose a new piece to work on.

YOUR ASSIGNMENT: Write a complete first draft of the piece you've chosen to work on. Follow the tips and guidance in this step.

Steps 11–16 will also help you with the writing of this initial version of your piece.

STEP 11

Fantasize

Most of us spend quite a bit of our time fantasizing. In fact, by the time we reach adulthood, we've become experts at it. Virtually anything that's pleasurable or painful can get our imaginations going. So can the *lack* of stimulus: When we're bored, we daydream.

This ability to imagine and fantasize can sharpen and strengthen your writing, and can add impact, insight, and intensity to it. And because this ability comes so naturally, you can put it to work in your writing quite easily. Often all you need to do is let your mind wander and follow it wherever it goes—or, at most, ask yourself a simple but provocative question.

Suppose, for example, that in your first draft of a short story, you've written a scene in which your narrator visits her seriously ill grandmother in the hospital. You could simply describe the sterile hospital room and leave it at that. But what if, instead of merely describing what you see in your mind, you let go of your mental reins and let your imagination lead you? Here are two different examples of what you might come up with:

(1) She seemed tiny and shrunken in the big, tightly-made hospital bed. Her face was damp with sweat, but someone had tucked the blanket under her chin, as if to hold her in place. The bed looked like a huge mouth waiting patiently to swallow her.

(2) The room was small, dark, and uncomfortably quiet. Ellen lay asleep in the bed, breathing shallowly, as if even while unconscious she was afraid to disturb the dark, heavy

silence. I pictured the room slowly shrinking with each passing hour, her breath growing steadily shallower, until at last the darkness and silence were complete, and the room had become a coffin.

In each of these cases, I first created a basic setting, then allowed my mind to play with it, alter it, and fantasize about it. The result in each case was an unusual and—I hope—disturbing image.

Fantasizing doesn't only lend itself to the writing of fiction and poetry. It can be just as powerful a tool if you're creating analytical, down-to-earth non-fiction. Consider the following example, noting in particular the final image:

> Despite his insistence that balancing the state's budget would be a top priority during his first term as governor, in his very first year in office he supported a $52 million increase in state spending. His compatriots argued that this increase was actually quite modest, since the state's total budget has exceeded $15 billion each year for over a decade. But consider this: if 52 million dollars in pennies were placed atop the State Capitol building, the Capitol dome would immediately crumble under their weight.

Fantasizing often works by adding a twist—a new perspective, approach, connection, emphasis, or association.

One of the best ways to fantasize as you write is to ask yourself the question "what if?" The potential variations on this question are limitless. Some examples: "What if she had arrived ten minutes earlier?" "What if he hit her instead of kissed her?" "What if this had happened during medieval times?" "What if the doorbell were to suddenly ring—and who would it be?" "What if she saw a galloping horse instead of a trotting dog?" "What if his 'skiing accident' were actually a self-inflicted injury?" "What if it were night?" "What if Nathan was poor instead of well-to-do?"

"What if this were narrated by Gwendolyn instead of written in the third person?" "What if this had taken place in a matriarchal culture?"

You've been developing your ability to daydream and fantasize all your life. With a little practice, you'll soon be able to use this skill to make your writing stronger and deeper.

YOUR ASSIGNMENT: As you create your first draft, let your imagination loose. Instead of writing what's most likely to happen next, or the image your reader is most expecting, give yourself free rein to visualize, to imagine, and to dream.

If your ability to fantasize doesn't kick in automatically, ask yourself one or more of these questions:

- What's the best thing that could happen in my piece right now? The most exciting? The most appropriate?
- What's the worst thing that could possibly happen now? The most painful? The most unlucky? The most dangerous? The most frightening?
- What is the single most unexpected thing that might happen now? The strangest? The most incongruous? The most absurd?
- What's the funniest thing that could happen right now?
- What does the person, object, image, or action I'm writing about remind me of? How? Why?
- What if _____ (fill in the blank yourself)?

As you write, you're by no means obliged to use whatever fantasy or fantasies you come up with. If what you visualize doesn't feel right, simply ignore it, and begin fantasizing in another direction—or, if you prefer, ask yourself a different question.

STEP 12

Combine Diverse Elements

One of the very best ways to intensify, vivify, and energize your writing is to bring together two or more different things that wouldn't normally be associated with one another. The late Arthur Koestler called this process *bisociation,* and it is one of the simplest and most effective writing techniques.

Here are some examples of bisociation:

- A snowman in a tanning booth.
- A sign in the window of a funeral home that reads: "Today's special: free toaster with every cremation."
- This line in a poem: "When you left, cutting the roots of your promise,"
- This paragraph: "All I ever really wanted in life was to dress in white and be surrounded by bright light. *I should have become a Hindu,* I thought, *or a dentist.*"
- A race of highly-intelligent, technologically-advanced aliens from another planet, all of whom move their lips when they read.

Even titles can be examples of bisociation. Consider Mark Twain's *A Connecticut Yankee in King Arthur's Court* or Toni Cade Bambara's *Gorilla, My Love.*

Then there is *trisociation,* which is the bringing together of *three* diverse elements into a single event, image, situation, or idea. Here's an example of a trisociative premise for a poem or story: A professional bowler has a profound spiritual experience, becomes an itinerant Zen monk, and dedicates her life to driving her Winnebago from one bowling alley to another, teaching bowlers how to become one with the pins. (The first line of such a piece might be, "Buddha would have made a great bowler.")

Why are bisociation and trisociation so powerful and effective? Because they enable readers to look at things in new ways, to see (or imagine) connections and relationships that they wouldn't normally see. Bisociation thus widens and deepens your readers' vision of the world.

Not only can bisociation make your writing richer and deeper for readers, but the act of bisociating can help *you* to see things in new and different ways. Bisociation can lead you deeper into your piece—and into your own heart and mind—by transforming and expanding your vision.

Bisociation doesn't have to be as obvious or overt as in the above examples, however. There are other, more subtle ways in which two or more elements can be combined to add strength and vision to your work. Often, in fact, the act of bisociation can be completely invisible to readers.

You might, for example, combine the attributes of two or more different places to create a new setting more vivid and moving than any of the originals. Suppose that you're writing a poem in which the daughter of a retired steelworker walks through an abandoned steel mill. Perhaps you've wandered through several abandoned factories yourself over the years, and you've accumulated quite a mental library of images from them. Instead of simply choosing one specific factory as the setting for your poem, you might pick the ten most striking images and combine them into a single (fictitious) setting. If you like, you can of course add entirely made-up images as well.

Here's another example. You might choose to combine the personality traits of several different people you know to create a single character. Suppose that you're writing a story about a young policewoman's first day on the job. You might give her the quick, stiff movements of your mother, the anxious grimness of your cousin Terry, your neighbor's compulsive gum chewing, and the low-key deadpan humor of your best friend's gardener—as well as a variety of other traits of your own invention.

Here's a third example, this one combining incidents and events. Suppose you're writing an essay about how American elementary schools have changed very little over the past 40 years. In relating a typical day in a third-grade classroom, you might blend some incidents from your own childhood, an anecdote from a recent newspaper article, and stories told to you by your brother, your boss, and several schoolteacher friends.

Two of the examples above—the ones that create a place (the abandoned steel mill) and a character (the rookie policewoman)—demonstrate an additional form of bisociation: they combine the real and the imaginary. This melding of memory and imagination often results in some of the strongest, most moving writing.

YOUR ASSIGNMENT: As you compose your first draft, look for opportunities to make connections and associations through bisociation and trisociation.

One excellent way to do this is to keep all your responses to the assignments in Step 7 near you as you write. Scan these briefly at opportune moments, such as:

• Before each writing session.
• If you're unsure what to do or where to go next.
• If you find your piece starting to fall into a clichéd or predictable pattern.

- If your writing starts to feel flat or low on energy, or seems to be going nowhere.
- If you find yourself beginning to lose interest in your piece.

When an example of bisociation or trisociation works, you'll know it immediately, because the connection will leap out at you in a way that's both surprising and satisfying.

STEP 13

Exaggerate, Embellish, and Enlarge

It's been said that all good writing tells the truth—not always the literal truth, of course, but some emotional or perceptual truth. When Dylan Thomas wrote of "the force that through the green fuse drives the flower," he was describing in poetic terms the inexorable life force that compels each living thing to survive and grow. Thus he was expressing a truth using words that, if taken literally, would seem absurd and patently untrue.

Of course, it doesn't even occur to us as we read this line of poetry that Thomas was speaking in any way other than metaphorically. We don't expect a completely literal and realistic description because we're reading a poem, not a news article.

We grant this freedom—the freedom to abandon the literal truth in order to express emotional or imagistic truths—not only to poets, but also to fiction writers, playwrights, and other creative writers. We allow these people to rewrite reality, to stretch the truth, and even to lie, so long as what they write moves us, entertains us, or fulfills us in some way.

What does all of this mean to you as a writer? Just this: as you write your piece, feel free to lie, to exaggerate, to blow things out of proportion, to go to extremes, to pretend, to play, and to be outrageous. In fact, in creative writing (as opposed to reporting), virtually anything goes, so long as it has the *feel* of truth to it—that is, so long as it moves your readers.

Actually, much of the world's best writing is based on exaggeration, embellishment, and altered reality. Think of the work of Edgar Allan Poe or Sylvia Plath; George Orwell's *1984*; Miguel de

Cervantes' *Don Quixote*; Margaret Atwood's *The Handmaid's Tale*; or Gabriel Garcia Marquez's *One Hundred Years of Solitude*. Or think of *Moby-Dick*—a novel so outrageous that, when it was first published, two different reviewers insisted that Herman Melville was insane and needed to be locked up.

As a creative writer, you have enormous freedom—freedom to do whatever moves your readers, no matter how far removed from conventional reality it may be. This means that you have a license to lie—and, at the same time, the paradoxical responsibility to tell the emotional truth.

As your first draft progresses, feel free to make things bigger, or smaller, or faster, or scarier, or more painful, or more pleasurable, or stranger than they ordinarily are (or would be). If you originally envisioned a man with a missing toe, ask yourself if it would be better if he were missing a foot, or a leg. If you're basing your piece on a real-life incident which began with a knock on the door, maybe the door should instead be flung open, or go up in flames. If your original plan was to show 40 school children splashing in a pond, consider putting something else in the pond with them—perhaps their school bus, stopped at the pond's edge in a foot of water; or several mating dogs from a nearby farm; or thousands of chunks of ice from a sudden summer hailstorm; or half a dozen rusting gumball machines, dumped from the bridge above several months before.

One excellent way to add power and focus to a piece is to give it an extra twist or turn—to take things one step further, push the tension one notch higher. In doing so, you may find yourself naturally fantasizing, bisociating, or combining the unreal with the real.

Surprising as it may sound, the above advice applies to most non-fiction just as much as it does to fiction, poetry, and drama. It's quite permissible to exaggerate or bend the truth in most articles and essays, provided that you indicate clearly (at least via context or implication) that you're doing so. Consider this example from an essay by Lewis H. Lapham, noting in particular the final sentence:

> The bleak comedy of the autumn presidential campaign followed from the attempts to fit the candidates—both of them nervous government clerks—with the masks of wisdom and power. At their respective nominating conventions in New York and Houston, [then-] Governor Clinton and President Bush dutifully invoked the holy names of God and Elvis Presley, but it was clear from the tenor of their remarks that as between the two deities they placed their greater trust in the one with the rhinestones and the electric guitar. It was equally obvious that neither they nor their stage managers would have had much trouble with the question of endorsements. Offered a choice of photo opportunities, they plainly would have preferred to appear with the king at Graceland than with Christ at Golgotha or Gethsemane.

This freedom to exaggerate does not apply, however, to news articles, corporate reports, or other pieces where your responsibility as a writer is to present the facts as clearly and objectively as possible.

While having a license to lie allows you to try almost anything, it *doesn't* mean that whatever you try is always going to work. If you push things too far, you can undermine your piece. You can become absurd or silly when you mean to be dramatic; your characters can start to border on stereotypes or caricatures; you can undercut instead of heighten your impact, emotion, or mood; or you can simply lose your reader's trust or interest. (Remember, though, that you're only writing a first draft; if you *do* go too far, you can always scale things back or rewrite that portion of your piece later.)

While it's fine to exaggerate and embellish the people, settings, objects, images, and events in your writing, the one thing you should *not* normally embellish is your writing style. Good writing is as clear, concise, simple, and straightforward as possible. This is true of all forms of writing, including—perhaps especially—poetry.

As you write your first draft, avoid verbal tricks, gimmicks, and flourishes unless they are genuinely essential to what you are trying to do. Use standard English except when you have good reason not to; and when you *do* have good reason not to (for example, when you're working with certain metaphors, connections, leaps, dialects, dialogue, or direct quotations), bend the rules only as much as you have to.

None of this means, by the way, that you *have* to play fast and loose with objective reality as you write. It's possible to write an excellent poem, story, or essay by adhering strictly to everyday events, expectations, and language. Indeed, many excellent pieces do nothing more than relate actual experiences and incidents.

One more point about embellishment. As novelist Donald Westlake has pointed out, "The fictioneer labors under the restraint of plausibility; his inventions must stay within the capacity of the audience to accept and believe. God, of course, working with facts, faces no such limitation." Often our everyday reality can seem so strange, so rife with coincidence and connections, or so perfectly arranged and plotted out, that if you were to simply report the events that took place, no one would believe you. You'd be accused of heavy-handedness, of factitiousness, or of manipulating your characters (and, perhaps, your readers). In these cases, you may need to *de-embellish*—that is, tone down or rewrite what actually happened in order to make it believable to your readers. This may feel awkward at first, but in fact what you're doing is no different from making things larger than life: you're presenting images, ideas, and events in an amended way so that they authentically express emotional and perceptual truths.

YOUR ASSIGNMENT: In your first draft, feel free to play with the truth. Deliberately veer away from what your reader might expect or consider normal. Exaggerate, lie, or make up things; alter, twist, or transform reality. Skew things, turn them on their sides, or change some of their essential qualities.

If, as you write, you find your piece beginning to lose energy, become predictable, or feel sluggish, perhaps a slight (or more than slight) change of direction is what you need. Follow the suggestions in this step, and see where your efforts take you.

STEP 14

Engage Your Reader's Senses

Our senses are the instruments through which we perceive the world. In fact, it is only through our powers of sight, hearing, touch, smell, and taste that we can connect with reality. Our perceptions provide us with information that enables us to construct a multi-sensory picture of the world inside our heads.

This has profound significance for us. *As creative writers, whose only tools are words, we must create (or recreate) the world inside our readers' heads.* In order to create this mental world, we must therefore give our readers sensory information; we must describe everything in terms of what we can smell, hear, touch, see, and taste.

Each set of related sensory details is called an *image*. Most of us tend to think of images as visual—red and yellow streamers blowing in a breeze, morning fog rising from a lake, or a dog baring its teeth. But images can involve *any* of the senses—the tremolo of a loon, the smell of burning leaves, the smooth, cool texture of marble, and the sharp, sweet taste of licorice.

An image can also combine two or more different senses. Some examples: ten elderly women laughing and splashing each other in a heavily-chlorinated swimming pool; a wet, mewing kitten trying to climb your bare leg, its tiny claws digging into your skin; a perky, smartly-dressed department store manager giving a pep talk to three dozen novice Santa Clauses. Combining information from two or more different senses often creates the most vivid images and results in the most intense and affecting experiences for readers.

Although most of us have been taught to respond primarily to visual imagery, our most acute and powerful sense is actually our sense of smell. Many of our strongest memories are of odors and aromas, and often a single smell can evoke several vivid and highly-detailed recollections or images. For example, the smell of cotton candy always evokes (for me, anyway) strong, clear images of an amusement park on a hot summer day.

It's not enough to simply provide sensory information, however; you must provide the specific, accurate information that captures and conveys the essence of what you're describing. *Knowing how to pick just the right sensory details is at the heart of good writing.* This is easier to do than it sounds—in fact, most of us do it every day in our speaking and thinking.

For example, let's consider the object I'm looking at right now. If I told you it was ugly and boring but functional (and it is all three), you'd have no idea what it is. But if I said that it squats in the corner of my office, gurgling, hissing, and giving off heat, chances are that you would correctly identify it as a radiator. You are able to do this because I gave you specific information about how it looks (it "squats in the corner of my office"), what it sounds like ("gurgling, hissing"), and what it feels like ("giving off heat")—and you used that information to create a multi-sensory picture in your mind.

This worked because I gave you in words the same sensory information you would receive directly if you were observing the radiator yourself. More important, I selected the *right* pieces of sensory information, the ones that enabled you to form a complete mental picture. I could just as accurately have described the radiator as a solid, heavy object with gray peeling paint and a knob on one end, or as a four-legged set of pipes held together with a threaded metal rod—but none of this information would have captured the essence of what a radiator is.

Let's return for a moment to my first description of the radiator. In this description I used the words *ugly, boring,* and *func-*

tional, none of which are very helpful. In fact, these words don't really describe the radiator in my office at all; instead they describe *my judgments about* the radiator.

No object or person is inherently ugly, boring, or functional. After all, a painting that one person finds ugly another may think is beautiful. I enjoy Terry Gilliam's films a great deal; my wife finds most of them only passably interesting. And while I might say that our cats are functional because they kill mice that get into our home, do they stop being functional when all of the mice have been killed?

There's nothing wrong with making such judgments, of course, or with including them in your writing. But don't confuse judgments with sensory details. Look at the two lists of words below:

tingling	fantastic
ochre	harmonious
mossy	attractive
stiff	unappealing
cracked	unique
sweating	nasty
bitter	ordinary
screeching	delicious
musky	miserable

Each of the words in the left-hand column provides specific sensory information, through which your reader can create a clear mental picture. In contrast, all the words on the right represent someone's evaluation, opinion, or judgment. They are one step removed from actual sensory experience.

If I tell you I ate a delicious lunch this afternoon, you'll have no idea what I ate. It could be pizza, chowder, or Caesar salad. I haven't really shown you *anything* about my meal—I've only told you my opinion of it. But if I say, "I had deep-fried bean curd with sautéed broccoli and roasted cashews in garlic sauce," not only do you know exactly what I ate, but you'll have some idea what it looked, smelled, and tasted like, because I've given you enough sensory details to create a picture in your mind. I've also allowed you to have your own opinion of bean curd, which you may not think of as delicious.

I don't mean to give you the impression, however, that the more sensory details you provide, the better. It's not really a question of amount, but of appropriateness. To paraphrase one of Douglas Adams's characters, you need to put in the right bits and throw the other bits away.

Consider this sentence: "Taking the long, sharp, gleaming metal hoe, she planted her bare feet firmly on the dusty path, inhaled noisily—the phlegm in her sinuses making her wheeze a bit—and struck the green, slithering snake just behind its slightly uplifted head." This sentence is so overloaded with sensory information that you don't know which details to focus on, or which ones are meant to be significant. The trick is to provide the most important or significant details—the ones that reveal the essence of the person, object, action, or situation at hand.

When you present your reader with sensory information, you *show* them people, objects, settings, and events, rather than merely tell about them. Consider the following two passages:

(1) Shannon was excited.

(2) Shannon pushed her way to the front of the cheering crowd. She knocked a string of balloons off a table, climbed on top, and shouted, "It's a goddamn miracle!"

The first sentence *tells* the reader how Shannon feels, but fails to bring the reader into the scene; the second *shows* the reader exactly what's happening, and allows them to see, feel, and even share in Shannon's excitement.

Notice, by the way, that in the second passage the word *excited* doesn't appear anywhere. There's no need for it. Because the passage *shows* the reader clearly what Shannon is doing, her emotions come through loudly and clearly.

In creative writing, showing is almost always preferable to telling, unless you are trying to make a quick transition from one scene, time, location, viewpoint, or topic to another.

Incidentally, everything I've written in this chapter applies as much to a piece of nonfiction as it does to a work of poetry or fiction. To see how these principles work in nonfiction, let's look at a few sentences from one of Annie Dillard's non-fiction books, *The Writing Life,* in which she observes the flight of a sphinx moth:

> After trembling so violently that it seemed it must blow apart, the moth took flight. Its wings blurred, like a hummingbird's. It flew a few yards out over the water before it began losing altitude. It was going down. Its wings buzzed; it gained height and lost, gained and lost, and always lost more than it gained, until its heavy body dragged in the water, and it drowned before my eyes with a splash.

No matter what genre you are working in, the more you focus on providing the right sensory details—and the more that you are specific, clear, and concrete—the more likely you are to engage and affect your readers.

YOUR ASSIGNMENT: As you write, imagine that what you're writing about is actually happening, right before you, right now. Play it out inside your head, as if it were a movie. Follow it from beginning to end, moment by moment, and write down what you observe—what you hear, what you see, and, if appropriate, what you smell, taste, or touch. Focus on sensory details, and try to home in on just the right ones.

Don't expect to be able to do this well in every line or sentence, however. Finding the right details or images doesn't always come easily, especially in a first draft. If, as you write, an image that fits or feels right doesn't come, don't stop writing. Leave a blank space, or make some notes, or temporarily use an image that's not quite right; then move on. Only later, once your draft is complete, should you come back and work on that image further.

Also as you write, show things to your reader rather than merely tell about them. This is particularly true in the case of emotions. Instead of writing *I was furious*, show yourself being furious. For example: *"Forget it!" I shouted, grabbing my books. I stormed out of the bedroom, slammed the door behind me, and ran down the steps before I could have second thoughts.*

Your ability to find and use the right sensory details will get steadily better with time and practice. And remember: you already use this kind of detail every day in your speech and thinking.

STEP 15

Avoid the Most Common Writing Mistakes

The mistakes I discuss in this chapter aren't errors of grammar, punctuation, spelling, or sentence structure. All writers make these small errors when they write, and since they're easily fixed with some careful editing and proofreading, they should be of no concern to you as you compose your first draft (or, in many cases, your second or third). It's more important to keep the words coming—so leave the fine tuning for later.

In this step I won't be dealing with problems such as wordiness, overwriting, unnecessary repetition, or awkward pacing, either. These, too, are all quite natural in early drafts. Because they're problems of degree or balance, they are rarely serious. Fixing them is much like adding flour to some tasty but runny pancake batter.

The mistakes I'm talking about here are basic—and potentially serious—errors of conception or presentation: They are problems that can point your piece in the wrong direction, undermine your basic intent, or confuse or alienate your readers.

In one very important sense, of course, nothing in a first draft is ever really a mistake, since you can always change it later as you revise. Indeed, sometimes it's downright necessary to write something badly the first time around in order to write it well the next. I frequently write first drafts in which very little works well, just to get some words, ideas, and images on paper. This initial draft provides me with a general structure and a set of working notes to help me write the draft that follows. Even if I end up using little or nothing from my first draft, writing it was nevertheless an essential part of my composing process.

There are, however a number of common traps that new writers (and many experienced ones as well) can frequently fall into. Being alerted to these problems in advance can be enormously helpful, because when your piece goes astray, you'll be able to catch yourself and redirect your efforts. Better still, you'll be able to avoid many of these problems in the first place.

As you write, keep an eye out for these all-too-common pitfalls:

- **Trying to do or say too much.** It's important to keep your focus narrow and specific in any short piece, particularly an essay. If you try to cover too much ground or jam in too many events or images, you'll confuse your reader and ultimately distance them from your piece. Don't try to sum up the history of Europe in a two-page poem, or discuss all the problems of modern life in a single brief essay, or squeeze three murders, a rape, and a robbery into one five-page story.

- **Dealing in universals or generalities.** While it's certainly fine to write about things such as love, greed, justice, war, or ignorance, writing about them as abstract entities rarely works, and usually results in distant, abstruse pieces that leave readers unmoved. On the other hand, you *can* move and involve your readers by focusing on specific examples— e.g., a particular act of love or greed, a certain battle or court case, or a particular person caught up in ignorance and forced to suffer its consequences. Each particular example then becomes emblematic or representative of the larger subject you're writing about.

- **Writing in expository lumps.** An expository lump is an overly-lengthy and detailed stretch of narration that provides extensive background or explains to the reader what is going on. ("The two women found themselves in this situation as a result of a bet the two of them had made six years earlier. Tanisha had claimed that women traveling alone were particularly vulnerable in airports, while Arlene had insisted that airports were some of the safest spots on the planet...") Usually an expository lump merely tells the reader what they should be shown instead. In most cases, an expository lump should be replaced with scenes or stanzas that reveal the same information in a more dramatic and sensory manner. Sometimes the information in an expository lump can be best revealed in bits and pieces throughout your piece, using narration, imagery, and dialog. And, occasionally, it makes the most sense to stick with a narrative explanation, but to shorten and simplify it greatly.

- **Placing a flashback near the very beginning of a piece.** This can be confusing and hard to follow, and editors see it as a sure sign of amateurism. (When some editors come upon a flashback on the first page, they immediately stop reading and reject the piece.)

- **Having characters explain things to each other.** This is simply an expository lump presented in dialog form. For example: "Well, Margot, as you know, we first took our jobs as cooks back in 1990, following that terrible accident in the elevator. After six months we started dating and eventually married. Today we work as chefs and live on Seventh Avenue." You can hear how ludicrous this sounds. Follow the advice in the expository lumps section above.

- **Using stereotypes or caricatures.** Good writing reveals or creates three-dimensional people. Resist the temptation to stereotype others, whether they're actual persons or fictional characters. Places can easily be stereotyped, too; if you're writing about Paris, mention more than just the Eiffel Tower and the Louvre. When describing any setting, don't be satisfied with just a few broad, familiar strokes.

- **Using anti-stereotypes.** Don't fall into the trap of simply turning a portion of a stereotype upside down. When you show your reader a macho football player whose hobby is crocheting, or a mousy wallflower who likes to go big game hunting, you're still describing people two-dimensionally.

- **Failing to use standard English.** Don't use buzzwords or technical language unless you have good reason to, or unless you're sure your readers will understand what you mean. And if you're writing poetry, remember that poems aren't supposed to be written in some special poetic language that's high-handed, intellectual, Shakespearean, or Biblical. Like all forms of creative writing, poems should normally be written in standard English. (Shakespeare's sonnets sound a bit formal to us now because they were written in the standard English of Shakespeare's time.) You *can* alter standard English occasionally in poetry—and in fiction, non-fiction, and drama as well—but only when you have good reason to, and only when normal English won't serve your purposes as well.

- **Overtly manipulating characters and/or events.** Actually, it's fine to manipulate the people and events in a work of fiction, drama, or poetry—but it's important that whatever happens *seems* to be natural and appropriate. Do your directing from off-stage, as subtly and invisibly as possible. If your reader can clearly see you pulling strings, your piece will lose much of its impact; in fact, your reader may feel just as manipulated as the events and people in it. Rethink your plot, and come up with a more subtle or believable sequence of events—or more believable reasons why your characters act the way they do.

- **Stretching your reader's credulity.** Your reader must accept the reality of what you write—if not literally, then at least emotionally. When you play with your reader's sense of reality, you must do it in a way that they'll find emotionally believable. If you discover yourself asking your reader to make too big a conceptual or emotional leap, try replotting your piece, or making that leap smaller, subtler, or easier to handle.

- **Showing off.** Don't try to impress your reader with your cleverness, cuteness, or profundity. Your purpose as a writer is to move your reader, not to convince them of your ability or sensitivity. If something genuinely fits well in your piece *and* happens to be clever, cute, or profound, by all means use it. But if something isn't necessary or important to your piece, then no matter how clever or profound it may be, it will only distract or disorient your reader. Get rid of it. (But don't throw it away; file it somewhere, or save it in your notebook. You'll probably be able to use it later in a different piece.) If something can be done simply, do it simply. Don't make it unnecessarily complex, especially if the only point of the complexity is to flaunt your skills or insight. As Philip Roth has pointed out, writers often must work hard to make their writing look as if it came easily.

- **Being deliberately obscure or confusing.** If you think confusion and obscurity are desirable—and some new writers think they are, particularly in poetry—please think again. Being unclear isn't going to wow your readers with your brilliance; it's only going to leave them puzzled. (It's okay, of course, for a character you're writing about to be confused, or for you to use confusion or obscurity to set up a mystery—provided that this mystery is adequately resolved later in your piece.)

- **Rhyming unnecessarily.** About 90% of the new poetry being published today makes little use of rhyme. Nevertheless, rhyming remains as useful, dynamic, and creative a poetic device as ever. Like any poetic device, however, rhyme should be used only when it deepens or enlivens your poem, or is in some way intrinsic to it. Using rhyme arbitrarily can undercut the impact of your poem, or make it seem forced or silly. Don't assume that rhyme is necessary or appropriate just because you're writing a poem. And if you've started off rhyming and the piece doesn't seem to be working, it may be best to drop the rhyme altogether—at least in your first draft. After the initial draft is complete, you can then go back and, if appropriate, meld rhyme back in.

• **Overaccentuating rhyme, or using it as your sole poetic device.** It is not true that if you're writing a poem, rhyme is all you need—any more than if you're writing dialog, all you need are quotation marks. Rhyme is only one of a wide variety of poetic devices. (See Step 25 for descriptions of many of these devices.) If you find yourself focusing almost exclusively on rhyme, refocus your attention on meaning, clarity, and word choice, and make rhyme your fourth rather than first consideration.

• **Writing in greeting card language.** This can take several forms: insipid poetry based on clichés and platitudes ("A friend is a gift"); deliberate but unnecessary overemphasis ("I was so jealous I could have died"); substituting syrup for real emotion ("When she thought about Clark, Marla's heart pounded inside her like the urgent beat of a savage's drum"); and, particularly in material for children, gross cutification ("'Gosh,' thought Stripey the Tiger, 'I wonder if I could learn to sing all those nifty songs like Beaky the Bird?'"). Greeting card writing is based on stock ideas and images rather than on your own authentic interests, concerns, and emotions. If you start producing this kind of writing, look back at your responses to Step 7 once again, and bring your focus back to what's genuinely important to you.

• **Using clichés.** A cliché is anything trite and overused. Clichés are usually phrases ("Look out for number one," "It's your funeral," etc.), but they can also be images (a cheery soda jerk with a pointed white hat; a cat pawing at a ball of yarn), ideas (war is hell; Californians are laid-back), or even whole scenes (the lovers wake up to a magnificent sunrise). When you notice yourself writing a cliché, replace it with something fresh—or transform it using a twist, embellishment, or additional element. Use the tips in Steps 11 through 14 as guides.

- **Basing your piece on references to literature or art.** New writers sometimes think this is classy, clever, articulate, or profound—but it's usually just dull. Loading up your piece with literary or intellectual allusions isn't going to move your readers, even if they recognize all of them. Allusions alone don't make for successful writing any more than nice-looking menus make for good restaurants. Look for meaning *within* your piece—in your people, events, images, observations, and ideas. If you catch yourself focusing on other people's work or ideas, reorient your piece to what's important and meaningful to *you*. (Certain types of writing—e.g., reviews, parody, and literary criticism—are obvious exceptions. These pieces should, of course, focus on the work and thought of others.)

- **Using vague language.** Keep your words clear, specific, and concrete. "Janine was dressed differently" doesn't create much of a mental picture. But "Janine had taken off her jumpsuit and was now dressed only in a blue bikini and sandals" offers the reader a strong, vivid image.

- **Inadvertently changing your viewpoint, tone, or tense.** It's perfectly legitimate to change any or all of these. But if you find that one of them has changed without your conscious direction or intent, take careful note. Your subconscious may have changed it into the best and most appropriate viewpoint, tone, or tense for the piece (or for that part of it). Look through the rest of your piece and make adjustments as needed.

- **Using passive language.** Some examples of passive language: "Delivery was completed." "The message was received." "The changing of management is being accomplished." In passive language, nobody performs actions; actions simply get performed. Passive language usually sounds stiff, distant, weak, and bureaucratic. In contrast, standard spoken and written English is usually quite active. In standard English, people do things. Some examples: "I delivered the wood." "Sue got the message." "Our management's changing. Frank quit, and

Marguerite's replacing him." Each of these sentences is clear, concise, and straightforward. If you start to slip into passive language, translate the last passive sentence that you wrote into standard, active English. Then keep writing in the active mode.

- **Using other people's characters or ideas.** Unless you've been specifically authorized to borrow from others, don't. If you do catch yourself borrowing extensively, write that part of your piece again, this time drawing strictly from your own ideas, emotions, observations, and concerns. (It *is* usually okay to use brief passages, concepts, and quotes from others as examples in your work, so long as you credit the original authors. Indeed, I've done this several times in this book. However, any characters, fundamental points, or central ideas should be your own.)

- **Confusing automatic writing with free verse or stream of consciousness.** You may have heard of a writing technique called *free writing* or *automatic writing,* which involves writing down in a steady, unedited stream whatever comes into your head. This is a perfectly legitimate method for getting words onto the page or computer screen. However, it rarely creates a finished or nearly-finished piece, and doesn't always create a viable first draft. Often it results in a kind of pre-first draft—a set of images, lines, and working notes not unlike what you came up with in Step 7. That's fine, of course; this material can then be used to create an initial draft, or can be incorporated into it. However, beginning writers sometimes confuse free writing with *free verse* or *stream of consciousness,* which are two very different things entirely. *Free verse* is poetry written without regular rhyme or meter. Good free verse is nevertheless quite carefully structured, and it makes use of a variety of poetic techniques. *Stream of consciousness* is the representation of a person's thoughts in prose or poetry; it, too, is usually very carefully written and structured. Stream of consciousness can employ standard English (as in Nicholson Baker's *The Mezzanine*), or a kind of modified and somewhat ungrammatical English meant to imitate the direct flow of thoughts (as in William Faulkner's *The Sound and the Fury*).

YOUR ASSIGNMENT: As you work on your first draft, keep these potential pitfalls in the back of your mind. (If you don't consciously remember them all, that's fine, so long as you've read everything in this step carefully.)

If you sense that you're falling (or have already fallen) into one of these traps, read the appropriate advice in this step once again, and apply it to what you're writing.

Important: you don't *have* to fix each problem as you notice it. If you can make a change easily, without breaking your writing momentum, that's great. But if you catch yourself, say, using vague language and clichés, it's fine to simply circle the passages in question, write a note to yourself about it (e.g., "vague & cliché –fix"), and continue writing. Once your first draft is done, you can then return to those passages and work on them further.

STEP 16

Try Outlining, Netlining, and Plotting

One way to get started is to outline your piece before you write a first draft. For many writers, preparing an outline before they begin writing provides them with a focus, a direction to follow, or a blueprint to work from.

But if outlines are so helpful, why have I waited until now to tell you about them?

For one very good reason: outlining isn't for everybody. For some writers, outlines are confining and stultifying. They'd much rather just begin writing, letting themselves discover what they have to say as they write.

Outlining, then, is an option—but not a requirement.

Incidentally, I am *not* talking here about the kind of formal outline you might have had to write in high school, in which you organized an essay according to topics, sub-topics, sub-subtopics, and so on. You don't have to be that rigid or prescriptive. In fact, for your purposes, an outline can be any set of notes that sketches out the potential structure, plot, direction, themes, or movement of your piece. (If you do feel that a formal outline—with its categories and subcategories, and its use of the symbols I, II, III, A, B, C, etc.—can be genuinely useful, by all means create one.)

Here are some legitimate and useful ways to outline a piece of creative writing:

• A simple list (perhaps numbered 1, 2, 3, 4, 5, etc.) of topics that you're thinking of covering, key points you plan to make, or scenes, sections, or stanzas you plan to write. If you like, add notes or a description to each item.

- A narrative synopsis of your plot—in essence, a highly-condensed version of your piece, written in prose.
- A narrative description of what your piece will do or be.
- A flow chart showing the movement of events, characters, ideas, points, topics, images, and/or relationships, from the beginning of your piece to the end.
- A *netline* or *mindmap*. This is an ingenious form of outlining that focuses on relationships rather than on plot or sequence. A netline presents information visually rather than in a linear fashion. It often resembles a spider web or a net—hence its name.

To begin a netline of your own, start with a blank piece of unlined paper (or a blank page in your writer's notebook) and the set of responses from Step 7 that you've chosen to work with. In the middle of the blank page, write down what you think will be the central premise, point, image, intention, character, metaphor, or event of your piece. If the piece has more than a single primary focus or concern, note each one near the center of the page, leaving at least an inch between items. If you're not sure yet what will form the core of your piece, leave the middle of the page blank; about two inches from the center (in any direction), note the most important elements that you've come up with so far, again leaving an inch or so between items.

Then, further out from the center, write down other, less significant elements and impressions for your piece. If one of these relates closely to something already on the page, place it near that item; if it's entirely new or unrelated, locate it further away. As ideas and images occur to you, add them.

Continue this process, placing related or similar items together in clusters, until you feel your netline is complete—or until you've run out of ideas and images.

As your netline takes shape, relationships between many of its elements will emerge. Indicate these relationships by drawing lines or arrows between the appropriate items. If lines cross or converge, that's fine. Some items will quickly become hubs, with many lines or arrows radiating out of (or leading to) them.

As more and more connections emerge, you may need to relocate some items, and perhaps even redraw your netline entirely. You may also want to use a larger page—for instance, a page from an artist's sketchbook.

When your netline is finished, it will show you at a glance how all the major elements of your piece relate to one another. It may also reveal connections and relationships that you hadn't consciously realized were there.

Two sample netlines appear on pages 98 and 99. The first is for a short essay on prison overcrowding; the second is for a poem (which could just as easily be a short story) about a romance between a master chef and her assistant. As netlines go, they're both rather logical, orderly, and detailed; I've made them this way so that they're easy to follow, and so you can see just how helpful a good netline can be. Don't be surprised if the netlines you develop are looser, less detailed (at least in early versions), and more jumbled looking.

Whatever type of outline you decide to use, think of it as tentative. If, as you write, a new direction or emphasis occurs to you, feel free to try it out. If it works, continue to follow it; if it doesn't, simply return to your original plan. Also feel free to amend your outline as your piece (or your thinking about it) grows and changes.

Although outlines and netlines primarily assist writers in producing first drafts, they can also be useful in other ways. For example, you might write a draft or two first, and then prepare an outline or netline of what you've written already. This can help you to sort out your thoughts, and to see patterns and relationships that you might otherwise have missed. It can also give you a better grasp of where your piece is heading, how it is succeeding, and where it still needs work.

One writer I know finds it useful to prepare an outline or netline when she's lost or stuck in the middle of a draft. This enables her to see more clearly where the problems in her piece lie, and what she can do to get it moving again.

As you might guess, different writers find different outlining techniques most effective. Some writers employ a variety of approaches. For example, I will sometimes outline first, sometimes netline first, and sometimes start writing without any preparation at all, depending on what I'm writing and what my gut tells me.

All of the outlining tehcniques described in this step work equally well for stories, poems, essays, and other forms of creative writing.

YOUR ASSIGNMENT: This is the one step that's optional. It's a suggestion, not a requirement.

If you've not yet begun to write your first draft, try outlining or netlining it first, using one or more of the techniques described in this step. If you're not sure which approach to try, pick the one that feels the most comfortable, promising, or intriguing; if it doesn't bear fruit, try another. Keep your outline near you as you write your first draft.

If you've already written part or all of a first draft, try outlining or netlining what you've finished so far. Then look over your outline carefully. What does it tell you about your piece—and the elements that make it up—that you didn't know before? Do you see any new relationships, associations, or connections?

If your attempts to outline or netline your piece get you nowhere—or if the very idea of outlining makes you stiffen up—then skip this step. Write your first draft by letting your piece gradually reveal itself to you, one line or sentence at a time.

Netline #1:
For an essay on prison overcrowding

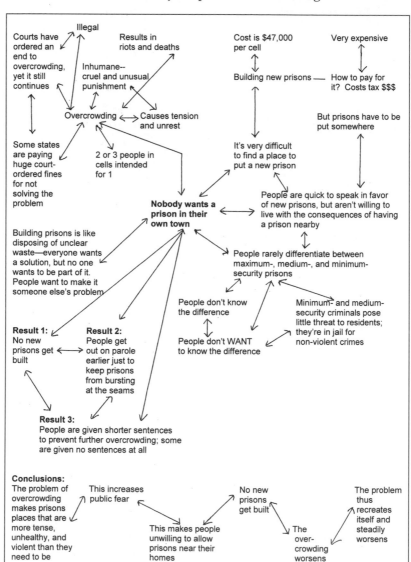

Netline #2:
For a poem or story about a chef and her assisant

Narrator is Susan, a middle-aged woman who's a master chef and restaurant owner. She hires Mario as her kitchen assistant. He's 29, just out of chef's school. His first career was as an accountant.

The piece focuses on their affair.

1. She interviews him for job, tells him her restaurant's her whole life, asks why he gave up accounting. He says, "I wanted to sink my hands into something. I wanted to honor my body and my tongue." She hires him.

2. Mario's smart and talented and quick. Too quick—his second day on the job, in a hurry, he knocks a handful of change into a mixer. He thinks he's got all the coins out, but next morning, eating a muffin, Susan bites into a quarter.

3. Five nights later, a huge group of very wealthy people arrives just before closing. They spend lots of money, love the food, stay hours past closing time, leave a $100 bill as a special tip for the chefs. She asks Mario, "How should we split this?" He suggests a bottle of Dom Perignon from the cellar, at cost. They drink it and get tipsy. He spills champagne on her neck, says, "If you close early you can lose your best customers." Leans forward, kisses her. They fall onto the counter, sending menus flying.

4. Their affair continues in the restaurant. They leave notes for each other on blank restaurant checks about when and where to meet to make love: *Party room, 2 p.m. Office, 11 p.m.*, the meat locker, the roof. On the roof, they picnic on paper-wrapped chicken, then let their clothing drop away. Afterward, she asks him to take her home with him. He balks. She forces the issue; finally he says, "I can't."

FOOD   MONEY   SLIPS/SHEETS OF PAPER   SPILLING/DROPPING   MOUTH/TONGUE

5. They close up the restaurant for the night; he kisses her and leaves. Feeling ashamed, she follows him home, already knowing what she'll find. From a distance, she sees his wife and children come outside to greet him, carrying what looks like a birthday cake. She drives away.

6. Next day, doing accounts, she realizes the restaurant's losing money. He appears behind her, places his hand on her shoulder. "I doubt you're breaking even," he says. "Too many cooks." She removes his hand, asks, "Where's your wedding ring? He steps back, shrugs. "I took it off to make sausage a year ago. Never saw it again." "Why did you seduce me?" "I wanted you."

7. Three days later he quits; he's taken a job as a sous chef across town. He tries to kiss her goodbye; she refuses, hands him his final paycheck. "You should have a professional look over those accounts," he says, and goes.

8. After interviewing people for Mario's job, she hires a talented middle-aged woman. She calls her second choice, a young man in his thirties, him apologetically that she's given the job to someone else. He thanks her, hesitates, asks her to dinner. He pauses again, asks, "Or are you busy cooking every night? "Of course not," she says. "Do you think this restaurant is my whole life?"

PART 3 Getting the Words Right

STEP 17

Look Over Your Work

Take a bow. You've done something that most people who want to write never actually do: you've written a complete draft of a story, poem, or essay.

This is a significant accomplishment—one that required vision, energy, and persistence. These are the same attributes that you'll use to complete your piece in the following four steps.

YOUR ASSIGNMENT: Strange as it may sound, your immediate task is to temporarily turn your attention to something *other* than your piece. In order to reread your finished draft with a fresh perspective and a clear mind, you'll need to distance yourself from it briefly. Spending some time away from your piece also gives your subconscious mind a chance to digest what you've done so far.

So take in a movie, read a book, go fishing, catch up on correspondence—or work on an entirely different piece.

Most writers find it sufficient to put aside what they've written for a few hours, or (more commonly) overnight. Others may need two or three days, or even a week. As you gain writing experience, you'll soon get a feel for how long you need to be away from a draft in order to see it through fresh eyes. For now, give yourself a minimum of a full day away from your piece—but no more than a week.

Once you've gotten some distance from your first draft, make yourself comfortable and begin rereading it. Do this *slowly, aloud,* seeing and hearing each word. Reading aloud enables you to absorb your piece through two different senses at once, thus doubling your perception and concentration.

Keep your original notes from Step 7 handy as you read your draft, and refer to them as necessary. If you prepared an outline or netline for your piece, keep this nearby as well.

Keep the following questions in mind as you read:

- What is this piece trying to do? (There may be more than one answer to this.)
- Does the piece *basically* succeed at what it is trying to do?
- Which parts or passages are generally successful? Which ones are not?

If something looks, sounds, and feels right as you read it, leave it alone—it's probably working well. But if your eyes, your ears, or your feelings aren't comfortable with a certain passage, it probably needs more work. Make a note to come back to it. (This can be as simple as circling certain passages, or putting a dot with a light-colored marker next to anything that needs changing.)

Please don't make any changes, even obvious ones, in your manuscript just yet. Simply indicate which portions or passages need attention. As appropriate, note what the problem or weakness is (e.g., "dialog seems too formal"), and what you think might be done to fix each problem (e.g., "relocate scene to shopping center," "find less obvious metaphor," etc.). When you rewrite in Step 18, you'll be returning to these passages and working on them.

As you read, also indicate gaps where things may need to be added, and cross out material that feels unnecessary or irrelevant.

If you feel that parts of your piece may need to be rearranged, make a note to this effect (e.g., "place after third stanza," or draw arrows). If you're not sure exactly what order the various sections should go in, simply write "reorder" in the appropriate spot(s), and keep on reading.

For the moment, ignore errors in spelling, punctuation, and grammar. At this stage, these errors are irrelevant, since you will likely be rewriting significant portions of your piece. You'll have a chance to deal with these small details in Step 19.

As you read through your draft, pay special attention to any images, ideas, observations, dialog, metaphors, descriptions, and other items that you feel work well. I suggest underlining each such passage and writing "good" next to it. This is important, because it demonstrates at a glance the strong points of your draft. When you rewrite in Step 18, these positive comments will help you decide what material to keep in. Furthermore, being able to see what you've done well will inspire you.

Once you've finished reading through your draft and making notes, take a break. (This can be as brief as ten minutes or as long as a couple of days; the choice is yours.) Then go back and reread your entire first draft again, aloud. Go slowly and take your time, just as before. Also as before, make notes on what works, what doesn't, and what you might do to improve the piece.

As you reread your draft for the second time, watch for some of the common writing problems described in Step 15. (You may wish review that step briefly.) If you notice your piece falling into one of these traps, make a note at the appropriate spot.

Chances are good that on this second round you'll notice things about your draft that you didn't catch the first time. Write down these observations. If you find yourself disagreeing with a note that you wrote when you first reread your draft, place a question mark above your previous comment. You'll have a chance to consider the passage further in Step 18.

If critiquing your own work seems difficult at first, or if you're not quite sure what to look for or write down, don't worry. Critiquing your work is a pragmatic, seat-of-the-pants process; there aren't any absolute rules or procedures to follow. You simply feel your way through it, line by line, using your eyes, ears, gut, and best judgment. As you become more experienced at writing, rereading, and rewriting, you'll get steadily better at knowing what works, what doesn't, and what needs to be done next.

When you've finished this step, you'll be ready—and well-prepared—to do some more writing.

STEP 18

Rewrite Your Piece

To *rewrite* or *revise* your piece simply means to make significant changes in it.

Most writers must do quite a bit of rewriting, revising, or revision (the terms are synonymous) on each piece they create, as well as some careful editing and proofreading, before they consider it finished. This is as true for experienced writers as it is for beginners. (For example, this chapter went through five drafts and a great deal of line-by-line editing before I felt it was done.)

Editing is the act of fine-tuning a piece—attending to its small points and smoothing out its rough edges. This means correcting word choice, punctuation, sentence structure, grammar, factual references, and other minor items. Don't begin editing until the process of revision is complete; otherwise, you're wasting your time, and possibly getting in your own way.

Proofreading is the process of checking for technical problems, such as missing words, misspellings, typographical errors, and so on. There is of course little point in proofreading a piece until it has been fully edited. (I'll discuss editing and proofreading in detail in Step 19.)

Revising and editing are fundamentally different processes, and you can't substitute one for the other. A piece with a flawed central premise, for example, can't be fixed by any amount of editing. Instead, it needs to be rethought and rewritten.

When you rewrite a piece, you may or may not complete additional *drafts* or *revisions,* which are new versions of your piece written more or less from beginning to end. Many writers find that they revise most effectively by writing a complete second draft, then a third, and then (if necessary) a fourth, until their piece is doing more or less what they want it to do. They'll keep their previous drafts close at hand, and as they write each new draft they'll incorporate the best passages and sections from earlier versions. Thus most of their revisions combine both new and old material, and each new draft represents clear, steady progress toward a goal.

Not everyone revises in such a linear, draft-by-draft fashion, however. Some writers will focus on one section, scene, or stanza at a time, going over that section repeatedly until they're happy with it, then moving on to another. (They needn't do this sequentially; they might, for example, work first on their ending, then on their beginning, and so on.)

The late fiction writer Sara Vogan used to rewrite by focusing on one specific aspect of a piece at a time. After writing her first or second draft, she'd go through it again to get the central metaphor working right; then she'd go through it once more, focusing on dialog; then she'd work with imagery and settings, then with pacing, and so on.

There are still other ways to revise productively. Some writers like to produce alternate versions of the same section or piece. For example, they might write four versions of the same poem, each from the point of view of a different character. Or they might write a dozen different scenes involving the same three people; then they'll choose the scenes that seem the most promising and build a short story around them. Or they'll start with a central premise and deliberately take it in several different directions, then work with the direction that most appeals to them.

Some writers use a combination of these techniques, tailoring the revision process to suit the particular piece and circumstances. For example, they might find themselves *redrafting* (that is, writing new drafts of) certain portions of their piece, but leaving other sections largely intact. Then they might create an interim outline or netline; then change the order in which the sections of their piece appear; then redraft some troublesome passages once again; and so on, until they feel their piece is ready for editing.

In short, there is no one right way to rewrite. Furthermore, since you don't have to write and rewrite in successive drafts, there is no "right" number of drafts that you should expect to complete. Each piece is different. The first piece that you write might require three full drafts and lots of section-by-section work. The next might emerge in first draft in near-finished shape, requiring nothing more than some snatches of rewriting here and there. The next piece might need half a dozen full rewrites, plus additional close work on many sections and passages. The next might require almost no revision in its initial sections, but a great deal in the rest. (Eudora Welty wrote that her stories typically required dozens of revisions; Samuel Beckett, on the other hand, claimed that much of his work came out full-blown in a single draft.)

You're finished rewriting when your piece's significant elements—its themes, ideas, central images or metaphors, pacing, characterization, tone, settings, dialog, etc.—all work well, fit together, and generally feel right.

In short, you can move on to editing when your piece consistently does what you want it to do—even though it may still have rough spots.

YOUR ASSIGNMENT: Put in front of you everything you've written on your piece so far: your notes from Step 7, your outline or netline (if you have one), your writer's notebook, a thesaurus, and your first draft. Place the draft in a very visible and convenient spot.

Now begin revising what you've written. Refer to any or all of the materials listed in the paragraph above, as you wish.

Some tips to keep in mind as you rewrite:

- Start by focusing on the largest concerns, such as your central character, premise, point, metaphor, image, plot, or theme. *After* you've got these major items working, then look at slightly less central concerns, such as overall structure, pacing, dialog, tone, secondary images and metaphors, and so on. (There's no point in tinkering with your dialog, for instance, when you need to completely replot your piece or rethink one of its major characters.)
- Don't fiddle with grammar, punctuation, spelling, or other small details. Dealing with these while revising can distract you from your piece's more serious problems. Furthermore, editing during the revision process is often pointless, since you might need to rewrite what you've just edited.
- Let your piece go where it seems to want to go. New ideas, images, and directions may reveal themselves to you as you revise. Neither accept nor reject any such possibility automatically, but evaluate each one on a case-by-case basis. If something feels right, be willing to use it, even if it means abandoning your original outline or intention. If this new approach ultimately doesn't work, however, return to your original plan.
- In revision, sustaining your momentum is not as important as it is when writing a first draft. If you get sidetracked or stuck, it's okay to stop and mull over options and possibilities.
- When you first begin revising, your piece may seem awkward, misshapen, or downright awful. *This is quite common for early drafts,* so take heart. As you rewrite, your piece will come more into focus and take shape. If a successful finished piece were represented by a perfect circle, your piece might look like this as you revise and edit it:

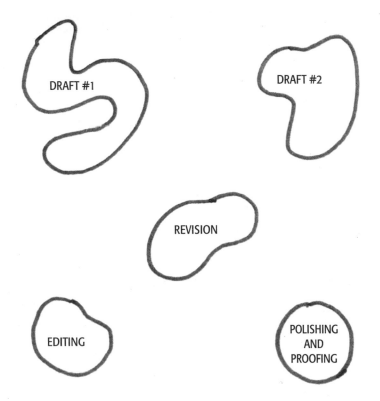

- Before you begin any new draft—or when you begin each new rewriting session—read over what you've done so far aloud, slowly, letting your ears and eyes absorb the words.
- Whenever you make a change, read it aloud a few times to see if it looks and sounds right. If it doesn't, the passage probably requires further attention. Similarly, if you've having trouble with a particular passage or section, read it aloud an extra time or two, looking and listening carefully. Sometimes your ear will pick up clues that your eye has missed.
- Many (but by no means all) writers feel that it's a good idea to take a break after each round of revision. This interval helps

them to clear their minds and bring a fresh perspective to their piece each time they return to it. Depending on the writer, this break might last a few hours, overnight, or a couple of days.

- One of the most important aspects of revising is cutting—getting rid of things that your piece doesn't need. These can be individual words or phrases; entire scenes, stanzas, or sections; or anything in between. Painful though it may be at first, cutting is an absolutely essential skill. Here are some things to keep in mind:

> ➤ There's an amazing amount of fat and repetition in virtually every essay, poem, or story in progress—so expect to do a good deal (or even a great deal) of cutting most of the time. Furthermore, expect to make additional cuts each time you reread what you've written so far. (When James M. Cain revised his novel *The Postman Always Rings Twice,* he ended up cutting out well over half of what he'd written.)

> ➤ Cut out anything that isn't genuinely useful to your piece; anything that doesn't support what your piece (or the appropriate portion of it) is trying to do; anything that does your piece more harm than good; and anything that isn't worth the number of words it requires.

> ➤ If you're unsure whether to leave something in or get rid of it, reread that section of your piece aloud. Do this twice—once with the passage included, and once without it. This should help you to decide which route to take. If you still can't decide, however, it's probably best to cut the material. As the old writing adage goes, "When in doubt, leave it out."

> ➤ If you can't get a passage or section to work right no matter what you do, consider cutting it entirely. Usually this will solve the problem completely, simply, and elegantly.

> ➤ Cutting doesn't just mean eliminating items. Sometimes it means combining or simplifying different elements or pas-

sages. For instance, you might reduce a wordy paragraph to a sentence or two; shorten a lengthy description to a couple of important details; compress two or three phrases into one; or replace a stretch of narrative (or even an entire scene) with a simple statement or transition, such as "Later, at the police station," or "That night, however, things went just as Kim had predicted."

➤ Occasionally something may strike you as interesting, insightful, or even brilliant—but it doesn't really belong in your piece. In such cases, *always cut it out.* If something doesn't belong, it doesn't belong, no matter how wonderful it may be. Put it in your writer's notebook, and save it for use in some other piece in the future.

• Throughout the revision process, your guiding principles should continue to be, "What moves, intrigues, or fascinates me?" and "What do I want to say, do, see, or have happen in this piece?" If you find yourself lost, stuck, or at a crossroads, ask yourself these questions. If you remain stuck, open up your notebook and look through it carefully. You'll probably find something in it that will add to your piece, redirect it, or get it moving again. If even this doesn't work, however, try out the strategies for getting unstuck in Step 10.

• Don't show your story, poem, or essay to anyone while you're revising it. Getting feedback from others while you're still rewriting and envisioning your piece can short-circuit your creative process. Instead, get your piece in the very best shape you can first; *then,* and only then, bring it to someone you trust for an evaluation. (One exception: if you find yourself utterly stuck and unable to proceed any further on your own—even after you've looked through your writer's notebook and tried out the suggestions in Step 10—then advice and criticism from someone else may help get your piece moving again.) See Step 21 for details on getting useful feedback from others.

- Occasionally, despite your best efforts, a piece simply might not come together for you. If, after several rounds of revision, your piece seems to be going nowhere—or if you simply lose interest in it—then your best bet may be to put it aside, at least for now. (But save everything you've written so far; you might be able to use it later.) If this is where you find yourself, then go back to Step 7 and pick a new piece to work on (and a new set of notes to work from). Using these notes, repeat Steps 9 through 18 for this new piece.

Step 18 can take a good deal of time, so don't rush through it. Revise your piece as much as you need to, keeping in mind that each time you go through it, you're bringing it one important notch closer to completion.

STEP 19

Edit and Proofread

Editing (sometimes called *polishing*) is the process of adjusting and fine-tuning your piece. It's the literary equivalent of adjusting the timing on your car, tossing a salad, or sanding and painting a bookcase you've just built.

As in rewriting, when you edit you'll add, replace, rearrange, and cut material. However, editing normally operates on a much smaller scale, focusing primarily on individual words, phrases, lines, and sentences, and only rarely on full stanzas or paragraphs. It also involves checking grammar, usage, punctuation, spelling, and stylistic unity (for example, capitalizing the first word of every line in a poem, or beginning each new section with an italicized heading.)

You should normally begin editing only when you don't need to further revise or rethink any significant portion of your piece.

A poem, essay, or story that is generally working well and needs no more revising may still require a great deal of editing. Sometimes a piece may even need little or no rewriting at all, but lots of close line-by-line editing. Indeed, several chapters in this very book were written in only one or two drafts, but required up to a dozen rounds of editing thereafter.

As you edit, pay close attention to rhythm, pacing, word choice, accuracy (as appropriate), and sentence and paragraph structure. In addition, consider your choice and presentation of each detail, image, and metaphor. If your piece is a poem, also look carefully at line and stanza breaks, physical layout and appearance, and sound devices such as alliteration, assonance, consonance, and onomatopoeia. (I'll define these sound devices, and others, in Step 25.) As you edit, read each passage aloud, looking, listening, and feeling for anything that isn't quite right.

With few exceptions, works in progress will require several rounds of editing. It simply isn't possible to catch and correct everything in a single read-through. In fact, you'll probably find that you can edit your piece half a dozen times or more, each time seeing or hearing problems that you missed before.

When your piece is as strong, as successful, and as polished as you can make it, it's ready for proofreading (sometimes called *proofing*).

Unlike rewriting and editing, proofreading is essentially a technical rather than a creative task. It's your final check to make sure that everything in your piece is complete and correct. This includes punctuation, grammar, capitalization, spelling, page setup, spacing, font and font size, and so on. When you proofread, you're taking a final look to make sure that everything in your piece is doing exactly what you want it to.

YOUR ASSIGNMENT: Reread your piece carefully—slowly and out loud. Make any necessary changes, cuts, and additions. After you make each change, read the edited passage aloud a couple of times to make sure it looks and sounds right. If it doesn't, keep working on it, or come back to it later.

When you've gone all the way through your piece, repeat the process to catch things you missed the first time through. If necessary, go back and edit it a third time—and, if need be, a fourth, and perhaps a fifth.

It is *not* normally necessary to take a break in between rounds of editing—but it's fine to do so if you like.

Continue editing until your piece is as effective and well-formed as you can make it. Keep the following guidelines in mind:

- Keep your early drafts, original notes, outline or netline (if any), and writer's notebook nearby. Refer back to any of these as you need to, especially if you're having trouble finding the right word, image, phrase, or detail.

- For many writers, a thesaurus can be absolutely invaluable during the editing process, so keep yours handy. (Don't, however, only use a thesaurus that's built into word-processing software, as most of these electronic versions are quite poor.)

- Cutting is as essential to editing as it is to revision. Be on the lookout for words, phrases, sentences, and lines that are unnecessary, or longer or more complex than they need to be. Be prepared to simplify, condense, and excise passages. Though it's unusual at this point, you may even need to simplify or get rid of entire paragraphs, stanzas, scenes, or sections. (Remember to save anything that's interesting, moving, or amusing for possible use later in another piece.)

- Watch for—and fix—words and phrases that are vague, unclear, confusing, clichéd, or unintentionally (and detrimentally) ambiguous.

- Make sure that any changes you made during the revision process are consistent throughout your piece. For instance, if you've changed a character's name from Marlene to Marion, make sure she's referred to as Marion at all times. And if you've changed the time of year from December to July, make sure that you've rewritten the paragraph in which Marion looks out the window at the falling snow.

- If you're not sure what word is best, what form of punctuation is appropriate, what rule of grammar or usage applies (or how to apply it), don't guess—look it up in your guide to the rules and conventions of English. (See Step 1 for a list of recommended guides.)

- All word processing programs have a spell-check function, and none of them works very well. Do use your spell-check, but also be willing to overrule it, or to cross-check words in a dictionary if something doesn't seem right. (My spell-check, for example, insists that shmooze and poststructuralism are not words.) If spelling is a particular problem for you, I suggest buying *The Bad Speller's Dictionary*, an inexpensive reference book that lists words alphabetically by their most common misspellings.

• Word processing programs are supposedly capable of editing, checking grammar and sentence structure, analyzing your style, and even critiquing your work for you. Unfortunately, they do not work at all, and are often laughably incorrect. (A grammar-check program once "corrected" the sentence *Where will we be?* to *Where will we are?*)

You'll know that the editing process is winding down when the number of changes you're making in each cycle of editing has begun to diminish. When, for two rounds of editing in a row, you make no more than a few small corrections each time, you're ready to begin proofing.

Another way to tell that you're ready to move from editing to proofreading is when your piece does what you want it to, sounds right when read aloud, looks right on the page, and feels right to you as well.

It's important not to let your eagerness to finish—or simple impatience or weariness—push you into declaring your piece ready for proofreading prematurely. Do whatever needs to be done—no less and no more.

Like revising and editing, proofreading is best done slowly and out loud. Use your ears as well as your eyes, so that one sense can catch what the other might miss.

I suggest proofreading your piece twice. Or, if you like, proof it once yourself and have someone else proof it as well; often a second pair of eyes will notice things that the first pair overlooked.

If the second time you proofread your piece you still find a significant number of items that need to be corrected, proof it a third time. Repeat this process as necessary until you can read your piece from beginning to end without finding a single problem or error.

Some writers, once they've finished proofreading their work, like to put it aside for a while—anywhere from a few days to a week or two. Then they read it over again with (ideally) a fresh perspective—and, if necessary, edit and proofread it further. This strategy isn't a required part of this step, but it is always an option. You always have the right to work further on any piece you've written—even if you previously declared it finished.

STEP 20

Find the Right Title

No essay, story, or poem is complete without a title. And not just any title, but the right title.

Sometimes the perfect title for your piece may leap full-blown out at you, or be so obvious that you scarcely need to think about it. In some cases, you might even know what your title is before you start writing. That's great, but relatively rare.

It's also possible to start out with *only* a title, which in turn will provide you with the inspiration or ideas for creating a poem, story, essay, or other piece. (That's exactly how this book came about.)

Often your title will emerge in the processes of writing, rewriting, and editing a piece. Sometimes, however, your title will need to carefully and patiently created, through conscious, deliberate effort.

Your title must genuinely add something to your piece, rather than merely restate it, describe it, or sum it up in some general, uninviting way. (Would you have picked up this book if it were called *How to Write* or *A Book for New Writers*?) A good title gives your reader a new (or wider) perspective, an extra thought or image, a twist, an irony, a bisociation, an additional metaphor, added emphasis, or some moving or thought-provoking counterpoint. Still more important, it does this in a way that deepens or strengthens the power of the piece.

When you're considering using a particular title, ask yourself if your reader will get more out of your piece with that title than without it. If the answer is yes, then you're onto something; if it's no, then the title simply won't do the job.

Some of the best titles are effective in two entirely different ways. Before you begin reading the piece, the title draws you in and prepares you subliminally for what you're about to read. Then, when you've finished reading and look back at the title, it resonates in another very different way.

Joan Didion's essay, "Some Dreamers of the Golden Dream," is an excellent example. It initially appears to be about idealistic people who resettle in California—the Golden State—where they hope to fulfill their dreams of a better life. By the time you've finished this grim and disturbing essay, however, you understand that Didion's California dreamers are out of touch with reality; they inhabit a mental world of movies, newspapers, violence, and greed; their dreams are psychotic fantasies. At this point you realize that the word "golden" in the title is heavily laden with irony.

Many good titles are deliberately catchy—e.g., Grace Paley's *Enormous Changes at the Last Minute,* Bill McKibben's *The End of Nature,* Harold Kushner's *When Bad Things Happen to Good People,* and Nathaniel Hawthorne's *The Celestial Railroad.* But catchiness isn't a necessity. Sometimes, in fact, a simple, restrained, understated title can be quite powerful, precisely because the piece it accompanies is anything *but* restrained or understated. Perhaps the best example of this is Shirley Jackson's "The Lottery." This brief story, written in a very straightforward, almost journalistic style, details an annual small-town lottery. At first everything seems quite routine and commonplace, but as the story proceeds, the situation becomes steadily more ominous, and eventually terrifying.

Good titles can also be ironic, as in Gwendolyn Brooks' "We Real Cool." This very short poem, written (in 1960) in poetic syncopation, is narrated by a Harlem jazz musician and pool shooter. He describes his and his cronies' lives in a total of eight lines, beginning with "we real cool"—but by line eight we've come to think of him as anything *but* cool. In fact, our reaction is pity.

Sometimes a title can be powerful and affecting because it can be read in two different ways at once, such as Eric Bogosian's *Drinking in America* or Alan Watts' *In My Own Way*. The further one reads in either of these books, the more the book resonates in *both* of the ways implied by its title.

Often a line, phrase, or quotation from your piece can serve as an excellent title, as in Flannery O'Connor's "A Good Man is Hard to Find," or the film *Lilies of the Field*. A title can also highlight a significant image or metaphor from your piece—as in, for instance, Sylvia Plath's *The Bell Jar*, Jerzy Kosinski's *The Painted Bird,* or Dylan Thomas's "The Peaches." (The title of Thomas's story seems quite flat at first, but takes on a great deal of unexpected meaning by the end of the piece.) It's also possible to draw a good title from an idea, setting, character, or other element in your piece.

The art of title writing hasn't been practiced as well as it could have been. A surprising number of very good works of literature—as well as innumerable not-so-good ones—have dull, simplistic, or unmemorable titles. Consider, for example, Poe's "The Raven" and Jorge Luis Borges' *Ficciones* (Spanish for *Fictions*).

Your title is what people are going to remember your piece by. Why not make it worth remembering?

YOUR ASSIGNMENT: Write a title for your piece—not just a decent or reasonable one, but the best and most appropriate title you can come up with.

If you already have a good idea what your title should be, wonderful. Jump down to the third paragraph from the end of this step, and follow the instructions for fine-tuning and refining it.

If you're uncertain as yet what your title should be, or if you have no ideas for it at all, then follow the guidelines that follow.

First, place your proofread manuscript in front of you. Also keep your various drafts, your notes, your netline or outline (if any), and your writer's notebook nearby, so that you can refer to any of them as you please.

Then read through your piece once more, at any pace you wish. This time you don't have to read it aloud. You don't even have to read every word; feel free to skim, or to skip back and forth among the various sections. As you read, look for key lines, concepts, images, metaphors, and bits of dialog. If you like, write these down.

For the next several minutes, let your mind wander among the various versions and elements of your piece. Look back through your early drafts and notes. See what clicks or connects, and write it down. Then work with these items until you've come up with a title that looks, sounds, and feels right.

Here are a few things to be cautious about as you work on your title:

- Don't be clever or elaborate just to be clever or elaborate. If a title doesn't strengthen or deepen your piece in some way, it's not right. (But save it in your notebook; you may be able to use it later with some other piece.)
- Avoid titles that are very vague or general, or that could apply to almost any piece of literature (e.g., "The Journey," "An Encounter," "Growing," etc.).
- Don't be too obvious or explanatory (e.g., "Jeremy's Sudden, Unexpected Suicide"). You don't want to telegraph a surprise ending, or give your reader so much information that they hardly need to read your piece at all.

In something as brief as a title, every word can make an important difference. Once you've got the right concept or focus for your title, you may still need to edit it in order to make it as strong and effective as possible. Consider all possible variations. You might need to choose the best form of a key word (e.g., "opening" vs. "open" vs "openings"). You might have to select just the right modifying words, or pick out precisely the right part of a pivotal phrase. For instance, once you're sure that your title will be brief, and will center on the word "exhibition," you may need to decide between "A Day at the Exhibition," "At the Exhibition," or simply "The Exhibition."

When you've got the right title for the piece, you'll know it and feel it.

STEP 21

Get Critical Feedback
From Someone You Trust

Once you've gotten your piece in the best shape you can, you're ready to show it to someone else. But not just anyone else—someone whose judgment you trust and respect.

If you're like many other new writers, this may be the most anxiety-producing of all the 30 steps, because you're making your piece—and yourself—vulnerable to someone else's opinions and judgments.

But listening to, evaluating, accepting, learning from, and sometimes rejecting the judgments of others are essential writing skills. Furthermore, feedback from someone you trust can help you see more clearly many of your piece's strengths and weaknesses—and notice others that you may have overlooked. Showing your work to someone else also gives you a chance to test market your piece, to get a sense (albeit a limited one) of how your readers may respond to it. Best of all, it provides you with an opportunity to improve your piece before you present it to the general public.

But what if your critic finds flaws in your piece, perhaps even serious ones? Then you've done exactly the right thing by getting their feedback. Using their most helpful comments as guides, you'll be able to strengthen and deepen your piece, and fix any problems you may have missed.

This assumes, of course, that you've selected a competent and compassionate critic. How do you find such a person?

Your ideal critic is someone who's intelligent, whom you trust and respect, who reads regularly, who is reasonably articulate, and who thinks much like you do. What's most important, though, is that they are naturally sympathetic to the kind of piece you've written. If you've written a mystery story, don't give it to someone who doesn't care for mysteries, even if they're your sister, best friend, or identical twin. No matter how wonderful a critic they might otherwise be, they're not likely to give you very constructive feedback. Find someone who likes mysteries instead.

Your critic doesn't have to be a writing instructor, a literature scholar, a published writer (or a writer at all), or a college graduate. They don't need to have a background in literature, though it certainly helps if they're widely read, particularly in the genre in which your piece is written.

Any one of the following people may be a helpful critic:

- A like-minded and intelligent friend, colleague, relative, partner, or spouse. This person is often your best bet.
- Another writer whose opinions (and, ideally, whose work) you respect.
- A writing instructor at a college, writers' center, or other institution. At some colleges, you can receive one-to-one criticism, and often academic credit as well, by signing up for an independent study project.
- An instructor at a writers' conference. At many writers' conferences, workshops, and retreats, manuscript criticism is included as part of the package; at some others, critiques are available for an additional charge.
- A writer-in-residence at a nearby library, writers' center, community center, or other community organization.
- A writing consultant or professional manuscript critic. These professionals normally charge $50-100 an hour, though I have recently seen as little as $35 and upward of $150. Some of these professionals charge by the page or piece. Writing consultants

and manuscript critics can be easily found on the web; start by visiting some writing-related websites, or go to Google and type in the phrases "manuscript critic" and "writing consultant."

Although some literary agents will critique manuscripts for a fee, in general I strongly recommend against paying a literary agent to critique your work. Agents are sales representatives for writers; thus they typically want every literary project to conform as closely as possible to whatever is selling well at the moment. As a result, many agents will respond unfavorably to a serious and ambitious literary project, but will give high praise to a glitzy but utterly predictable piece that's loaded down with sex and violence.

I also advise against having your work criticized in a writers' group until you're well along with Step 30. Although some of these groups can be quite helpful, they're primarily for people with a significant amount of writing experience. If you present your piece to such a group, members may give you feedback that's more sophisticated or complex than what you're ready for. Also, you run the risk of having your piece torn to shreds by a mean-spirited group member. This isn't such a big deal if you have lots of writing experience, but it can be painful and discouraging for someone who's just getting started. Certainly if a writer's group interests you, feel free to join (or create) one—but wait until you've completed at least 10-15 pieces and are regularly practicing Step 30.

Your critic must be able to be honest with you about your piece. If they can't be (or if you suspect they can't), find someone else. This is a particular concern if you're thinking about getting feedback from a friend, relative, partner or spouse.

Your critic should be clear about their own biases and have no agenda to push or axe to grind. They need to be able to look at your piece on its own terms—to see (and, ideally, appreciate) what it is trying to do and evaluate how well it is doing it.

Lastly, your critic should be specific and detailed about the various elements of your piece. Their comments should go well beyond "I liked it" or "I enjoyed the last several stanzas." They should be able to point to individual sections and passages and discuss clearly how they work—or how and why they don't.

Ideally, you'll be able to find a good critic from among the people you already know. If you need to look elsewhere, however, here are some suggestions:

- Call one or more of the following: the literature department of the downtown branch of any big-city library; the main office of the department of English, creative writing, or journalism at a university or college; the manager of a good independent bookstore (not a chain store); or the office of a writers' conference, workshop, studio, or colony.
- Contact one of the many writers' centers (also called literary centers) across North America. Many of these have working arrangements with manuscript critics. The center—and the critic—you contact do not have to be located near where you live. Good lists of writers' centers appear in many writers' websites; also search Google for "writers centers," "writers' centers," "writer's centers," and "literary centers."
- Check the display and classified ads in writers' magazines such as *Writer's Digest, The Writer, Writers' Journal,* and *Poets & Writers.* (Also check the websites for these publications.)
- Ask any writers you know for suggestions.

Before you hire any professional critic, it's important to learn something about their background and how they work. Here are some good questions to ask:

- How much experience do you have as a critic, writer, editor, writing consultant, and/or writing teacher?
- What work have you had published, and where?
- Are you interested in commercial writing, literary writing, or both?

- What types of writing (e.g., essays, science fiction, children's books, poetry, etc.) do you specialize in or especially like?
- What types are you unsympathetic to or less interested in?
- How do you feel about the genre in which my piece is written (e.g., poetry, mystery, fantasy, personal essay, etc.)?
- Will you point out both the weaknesses *and* the strengths of my piece?
- Will you not only show me where my piece needs work, but make specific suggestions for what I should do next?
- Will you consider my piece on its own terms, and base your critique on what it is trying to do?
- Do you plan to meet with me in person, speak with me by phone, provide a written critique, make line-by-line notes and changes on my manuscript, or some combination of these?
- What are your fees? Do you charge by the page, the project, or the hour?
- What do you estimate the project will cost?

If you have a preference for the manner in which your critique should be provided (for example, in an in-person consultation), clearly say so up front. Also let the critic know of any particular concerns you have or items you want addressed. For example: "I'm especially interested in your reaction to the scenes set in Atlanta. Do they work? And does the piece need all of them, particularly the first one?"

Feel free to talk with several people before making a decision. If you like, ask for one or two references.

Only work with someone who sounds sharp-eyed and honest—and whom you feel good about. Also feel free to work with someone on a trial basis at first—say, on one short piece or one book chapter. If you're happy with that person, you can then work together further; if you're not, you can shop for someone else.

Here is the single most important thing you need to know about receiving feedback on your work: you don't have to agree with your critic's evaluation or do what they suggest. And here's the second most important thing to know: if you don't agree, don't try to defend your piece or argue the point. Criticism isn't a debate. It's not the critic's job to convince you of anything, nor is it yours to convince them. A good critic will simply present you with their best analysis, observations, insights, and suggestions. It is then your task to listen alertly, take notes as appropriate, and consider carefully each of your critic's comments. If, after this careful thought, something makes sense to you, do it; if it doesn't, ignore it.

You may, however, explain what you were trying to do in a particular passage or section, and then ask, "Does it work? If not, why not? What do I need to do to make it work? Is what I'm trying to do worth doing at all?"

Now for the third most important point about receiving feedback: *never* do something to your piece that you don't agree with or believe in. Do what *you* feel is best, even if your critic was adamant that you need to do something else—and even if they've published 40 books and won the Nobel Prize in literature. After all, it's quite possible to be absolutely certain about something, yet wrong about it (I certainly have been). Furthermore, famous writers, literature professors, and even Nobel Prize winners can be just as fallible or short-sighted as anyone. Consider each comment you receive on its own merits, regardless of who made it. This applies to positive as well as negative comments.

Speaking of negative comments, these may hurt at first. But remember that these comments reflect only on your piece, which is still in progress—not on you as a person or on your ability as a writer. (If someone does say disparaging things about you or your overall writing ability, they're totally out of line. Find a different critic.) Also keep in mind that negative criticism will be much easier to hear and accept as you gain more writing experience.

Ultimately, only you can decide what advice to follow, what advice to ignore, and what changes (if any) to make in your piece. No matter what anyone else may think or say, ultimately every decision about your piece is yours and yours alone.

Will you always know what advice to follow and what advice to ignore? No. Will you always make the right decision? No again. But you *will* get better at both with practice and experience. And because writing is not like performing a flute sonata, you don't have to present your piece publicly until you feel it's ready. If at any point you realize that your piece needs further changes, or that something you previously disagreed with your critic about makes sense after all, simply revise your piece again.

Sometimes, when a critic points out a passage that needs further work and suggests a way to improve it, you may agree on the problem but not the solution. Often in such a situation you'll be able to create a solution that's far superior to what your critic suggested. This is actually quite common—after all, you'll usually have a vision of the piece that's bigger and more complete than your critic.

The guidelines in this step should help you to find a useful and effective critic. Nevertheless, since there are some second-rate (and even abusive) critics around, it's helpful to know what kinds of critical comments are *not* valid. Watch out for the following:

- Anything that makes a judgment about you as a person—e.g., "from the looks of this piece, you don't deserve serious criticism" or "only a crazy person could have written this."
- Anything that reflects negatively on your writing ability as a whole—e.g., "you don't have the stuff to be a writer" or "you should stick to writing short stories, because you don't have much talent as an essayist." Your critic has neither the evidence nor the right to make such a sweeping judgment.
- Any appeal to authority that is meant to supercede your own best judgment—e.g., "Well, the editor of *The Chicago Review* said exactly the same thing, and if anybody should know, it's him."

- Any negative comment about your work paired with a self-compliment—e.g., "Your dialogue doesn't sound real here, and believe me, I know, because I'm a dialogue expert." Your critic's real agenda may be to praise themselves rather than to help you.
- Anything that doesn't deal specifically with your piece—e.g., "Back in the sixties we used to sit around the Triangle Bar and think up ideas like these, just for fun; it was a lot more interesting to be a writer in those days."
- Anything that's vague or ambiguous—e.g., "I think you need to reformat this" or "There's something missing in this piece's texture." Ask for—and, if necessary, insist on—clarification.

If you'd like to get critical feedback from more than one person, feel free to. Indeed, a second critic may notice things that your first critic doesn't, and/or mayprovide additional fresh insights or perspectives. But keep in mind that no two critics will completely agree on almost any piece. In fact, experiencing such disagreement can help you to quickly get used to hearing, sorting out, and weighing differing opinions, then coming to your own conclusion.

If you decide to get feedback from more than one critic, *never* try to play one critic against the other. Don't say to critic B, "It's interesting that you think this section doesn't work, because critic A really liked it." Neither critic is going to feel very good about this. Listen to each person's comments carefully and thoughtfully; if need be, ask for clarification and details. Then make your own best decision.

YOUR ASSIGNMENT: First, ask yourself who you know who might be able to give you useful feedback on your piece. Make a list of these names. Speak with each person briefly; if they're interested in reading and critiquing your piece, ask them the questions on pages 126–7. Keep in mind that you want someone who reads and enjoys the type of piece you've written, who can be honest with you, whose opinion you value, and whom you feel you can trust.

If you can't find a good critic among the people you already know, follow the guidelines earlier in this step to find a talented and reliable professional.

If you want to show your piece to two different people, or even three, that's fine. For the purposes of this step, however, make three your maximum.

As you're getting feedback, listen carefully, and take notes if you need to. Don't argue or defend your piece. When you've gotten all of each critic's comments, thank them for their help.

Then spend some time looking and thinking over all of the feedback you've gotten. Consider each comment on its own merits. Be thorough, thoughtful, and careful. Decide which comments and suggestions genuinely apply to your piece and which ones do not.

Then repeat Steps 17–20; reread, revise, edit, and proofread your piece as necessary. Don't be surprised if this time around the process goes more quickly and easily.

When you've completed all this, congratulations! Your first complete piece of writing is finished.

You've accomplished a great deal so far. You've not only gotten started as a writer, but you've gone through every step of the writing process from beginning to end. Furthermore, you've created a full, polished, finished piece—and you've proven to yourself that you can do it. Give yourself a big hand.

What should you do with your piece now that it's finished? Anything you like. Give copies to friends, relatives, and acquaintances. If you wish, try to get it published by following the guidelines in Steps 26–28. Or, for the time being, simply file it away and move on to the following step. (Always save every piece you write, by the way—for as long as you live. You never know when you'll want to reread it, revise it, or try to publish it—perhaps years or decades from now.)

Everything you've done in the first 21 steps has served you well. Now that you've completed these steps, you have all the tools, talents, and experience you need to write a complete story, essay, or poem whenever you want to.

PART 4

Getting More Experience

STEP 22

Finish Several Different Pieces

In writing, as in so many other things, there's no substitute for hands-on experience, and no better method for learning and growing. The more writing practice you get, the better and more confident a writer you're likely to become.

You learned to write a finished essay, story, or poem by actually writing one from beginning to end. Now the best way to improve your writing and strengthen your skills is to write several more completed pieces.

This step will help you gain a wealth of writing experience—and build up a portfolio of finished pieces in the process.

YOUR ASSIGNMENT: If you're primarily a prose writer, repeat Steps 7–21 five times or more, in order to create at least five more finished pieces. If you're primarily a poet, repeat these steps until you've finished a dozen new short poems. If you work more or less equally in prose and poetry, finish three new prose pieces and six new works of poetry.

Follow the same process as before: begin by selecting a focus; next, write a first draft; revise your work; edit and proofread; get feedback from one or more people whose judgment you trust; then revise, edit, and proofread further. Repeat any of these steps as necessary.

Throughout your work on this step, continue to use your writer's notebook, both as a place to record strong images and ideas, and as a source of material for each new poem, essay, story, or other work.

In each of these pieces, feel free to work with whatever genres, forms, approaches, subjects, themes, styles, or ideas you wish. The choice, as always, is entirely yours; write whatever interests, moves, or fascinates you.

Because no one will see your work until you're ready to show it to them, you have enormous freedom—the freedom to try virtually anything you please. Don't be afraid to experiment, or to try out a variety of subjects and/or genres. If something works, great; if it doesn't, simply rewrite that piece or section.

If, on the other hand, you prefer to stick with one genre, a single subject, or both, that's fine, too. Concentrating your energies in a single direction often results in rapid, focused growth. If you write six science fiction stories in a row, for example, you'll probably have become a much better science fiction writer (and a better writer in general) than you were when you finished your first science fiction piece.

If you choose to specialize, however, make sure that you're not writing the same piece over and over again. It's easy for beginning writers to come to the same conclusion, make the same point, evoke the same range of emotions, or follow the same general plot in each new piece they write. Once you've written three different pieces, compare them carefully to make sure you're breaking new ground in each one, not simply writing variations on a single theme. If you *are* repeating yourself, make a point of deliberately doing something quite different in each new piece you write.

It's important that you get good feedback from at least one other person on each of your stories, essays, or poems. If you change genres, topics, or approaches, you may need to change critics as well. Someone who was your ideal critic for one piece (e.g., a political essay) may not be the right person to critique the next (e.g., a poem or a horror tale). Before you get feedback from anyone, even someone who's been an excellent critic of your work in the past, make sure that they're interested in and sympathetic to the type of piece you've written.

You don't have to write these new pieces one at a time. If you like, you can work on two or more—even several—at once. Many writers, however, find that they do their best work, and can most effectively focus their energy, when they concentrate on no more than one piece—or two, or three—at a time. With experience, and perhaps some trial and error, you'll learn what works best for you.

Remember that you can always revise anything you've written. Nothing you write is ever bad or wrong, but, at worst, simply unfinished. If part or all of a piece isn't doing what you want it to, keep working on it (or, if need be, put it aside and come back to it later) until you get it right.

Sometimes a piece simply won't come together for you. That's okay. This happens to experienced as well as not-so-experienced writers; in fact, for some famous writers, it happens quite often. If it does happen to you—or if you simply get fed up with your piece or lose interest in it—then don't be afraid to stop working on it. You can always come back to it in the future if you like. In the meantime, tell yourself that you've gotten some valuable writing experience, and begin writing something new. (Incidentally, the unfinished piece doesn't count as one of the five you'll need to complete in order to accomplish this step.)

Don't forget to save everything you write—finished or unfinished, successful or unsuccessful. Even an unsuccessful fragment may prove useful sometime in the future.

Each time you finish a new piece, congratulate yourself. And once you've completed this step, reward yourself with something you enjoy—a movie, dinner out, an afternoon off, etc. At the same time, tell yourself this: *you've now become a practicing writer.* Not only that, but with each new piece that you complete from now on, you'll become an increasingly-experienced one as well.

STEP 23

Read the Work
of Good Writers

Is it essential to read widely in order to write well? No, not really. But is it helpful? Yes, enormously.

Reading the work of writers you enjoy will provide you with specific, concrete examples of how good writing works. You'll have a chance to see a variety of approaches and techniques in action, and you'll be able to analyze how these move and influence readers. At the same time, you'll get to enjoy and appreciate what you're reading.

Actually, reading almost anything—even romance novels, popular magazines, and newspapers--can benefit your writing. *People* magazine, *Ellery Queen Mystery Magazine,* and *The Wall Street Journal* aren't likely to publish much great literature, but most of what they do publish is competently written and, thus, potentially instructive.

You may think that I'm going to trot out a list of specific books for you to read, but I'm not. In fact, I'm not sure it's fair to. If I've learned anything from 45 years of reading and 30 of teaching, it's that people's tastes vary widely. Clearly, there is no one book or body of literature that you *must* read in order to become a good writer. Furthermore, no one piece of writing has ever pleased everyone, or is ever going to. When it comes to both reading and writing, there is room not only for differences in taste, but for outright disagreement.

The guiding principle behind *30 Steps to Becoming a Writer* is to write what moves, intrigues, or fascinates you. Now let me give you some related advice: *read* what moves, intrigues, or fascinates you. It doesn't matter what literature professors or book critics or anybody else thinks. You're the one who's reading, and who knows better than you what appeals to you and what doesn't?

Here's another piece of advice: whatever genre you're working in (or plan to work in), read lots of material in that same genre. There's no better way to see what's already been done, what works, what doesn't work, what's currently being published, and what approaches and techniques are available to you. If you're writing (or interested in writing) fantasy stories, read contemporary and traditional fantasy. If you want to write travel articles and children's stories, look at some current travel magazines and some recent kids' books and periodicals. If you're thinking about writing a sonnet, look at what's been written before and what's being published now. (Yes, new sonnets—including some excellent ones—are still being published today in very respectable publications.)

Should you read any or all of the literary classics? If you like; it's entirely up to you. Reading literature that has lasted for decades or centuries can certainly help your writing, but it's by no means a necessity. (William Shakespeare managed to write quite well without having first read Mark Twain.) I suggest the following: try out some of the classic books and short pieces that look most promising to you—or that have been recommended to you by like-minded people whose opinions you value. If you find yourself enjoying something, wonderful. But if, after giving it a reasonable try, you're bored or turned off, put it aside and read something else. Don't expect to like (or dislike) any piece of writing just because of its reputation. Much of what's called great literature is seriously flawed, and some of it—in my opinion, at least—is downright awful.

How much reading should you do? It depends on how much time you have available. I suggest reading at least two books (or the equivalent in shorter work) per month. But consider that a goal, not a requirement.

YOUR ASSIGNMENT: This step contains five parts.

1. First, set aside some regular time to read—ideally an hour a day or several hours a week. If this is too ambitious—and for many people, it is—two to three hours of scheduled time per week will do.

It's important to specifically set aside this time, however—otherwise, it's likely to disappear in the flurry of daily obligations. Actually put it on your weekly schedule.

One excellent way to make time for reading is to unplug your TV—or at least redirect some of your TV and video-watching time to reading.

2. In your notebook, make a written list of some of the things you'd like to read in the months to come. You don't need to read everything on this list, and you don't have to go through it in any kind of sequence. However, whenever you're not sure what to read next, simply pick something from this list. Add to the list regularly in the future as new items occur to you.

What should you include on this list? Anything you've ever wanted to read but haven't managed to get to yet; anything that sounds intriguing or catches your eye; anything recommended to you by someone whose judgment you respect; and anything that seems potentially relevant to a writing project you're working on (or planning to work on). *Be sure to focus at least half of your reading in the same genre(s) in which you work (or intend to work).*

3. Spend some time browsing among the books and magazines at these four places: the largest library in your area (ideally, the main branch of a big-city library or the library of a major university); the biggest newsstand or magazine store near you; and the two largest bookstores you can easily get to. Bring your list of items to read with you. Wander among the shelves at your leisure, sampling whatever looks intriguing. Look at periodicals as well as books.

Do most of your browsing among the genres that most appeal to you, or that relate to the pieces you're writing (or planning to write). If you're interested in writing humor, look at funny books and magazines; if you're at work on several feminist essays and short stories, peruse feminist literature and magazines such as *Ms. Magazine.*

While it's okay to seek out specific titles, spend most of your time simply wandering, looking, and sampling, without a specific goal or agenda.

Give yourself plenty of time—at least half an hour at the newsstand and no less than an hour in the library and each bookstore. Write down the titles of any interesting-looking items on your list of things to read, and buy or borrow some of the books and periodicals that intrigue you the most.

Surfing the web is not an adequate substitute for this focused browsing. Do it in person, with books and periodicals you can hold in your hands.

4. Read some or all of the items you've acquired. If you find something particularly interesting, instructive, or inspiring, make notes on it in your notebook—or photocopy and save the appropriate pages. If something you read provides you with ideas, images, or inspiration for your writing, by all means use it (or note it down).

If you lose interest in something you're reading, put it down and read something else.

Remember that reading can also take the form of listening. Writers in virtually all genres regularly give public readings of their work at colleges and universities, museums, art centers, writers' centers, bookstores, coffee houses, bars, restaurants, community centers, and other public locations. These readings can give you an opportunity to sample other writers' work, as well as the chance to meet other writers in person. Many public readings are free, but many charge for admission.

5. Repeat parts two and three of this step at regular intervals—at least every 2-3 months.

Continue practicing this step indefinitely—not just until you finish this book, but for as long as you continue writing. Reading should be an ongoing part of your development as a writer.

However, don't let your reading cut seriously into your writing time. If your time is very tight, and you have to make the difficult choice between reading and writing, choose writing 90% of the time. While reading and writing reinforce and inspire one another, reading is never an adequate substitute for writing.

Furthermore, never read in order to avoid writing. Reading should support your writing, not get in its way.

Once you've completed this book, I suggest a change in how you continue to practice this step: occasionally include books and magazines about writing in your browsing and reading. Hundreds of useful and inspiring publications are out there—so browse, sample, learn, and enjoy.

STEP 24

Discover What Inspires You

In the first 23 steps you've gained a great deal of useful experience—experience in observing, reading, thinking, feeling, planning, outlining, writing, rewriting, editing, and proofreading. Now is an excellent time to review this experience and see what guidance it gives you for your future writing.

In this step you'll be reviewing your goals, your reading interests, your notes, your finished pieces, your work habits, and your overall process for writing. In particular, you'll be looking at what most inspires you to write—and at what inspires you to write your best work.

YOUR ASSIGNMENT: Get comfortable in your regular writing space; if you don't use one regular workplace, go to a spot where you particularly like to write. Lay out the following items in front of you: your notebook; the final version of each of the pieces you've written so far; and your working notes for each of these pieces (from Step 7). If you like, also lay out your outlines, netlines, and/or early drafts of these pieces.

Directly in front of you, place a blank sheet of loose paper. Write "Sources of Inspiration" at the top of this sheet.

Begin by reviewing your writing goals in your notebook. How many of these have you met so far? Which are you well on your way to attaining? Which are you still some distance from reaching? Now that you have a good deal of writing experience behind you, are there any goals that you wish to change? Are there new ones you'd like to add, or old ones you'd like to get rid of? How have your goals helped or hindered you? Has any goal gotten in your way—e.g., by being too ambitious? How can your goals be changed so that they inspire and energize you as much as possible? Write down any helpful changes, additions, or deletions on your "Sources of Inspiration" page.

Next, consider how and where you work. What about your workspace(s) has been most helpful and inspiring? Least helpful? Most distracting or difficult? What changes would you find most useful and inspiring? Should you rearrange the furniture? Move your desk closer to the window? Get a space heater to take the chill off? Replace that ugly poster? Add a floor lamp? Disconnect the phone? Be firmer with your kids about not interrupting you? On your "Sources of Inspiration" sheet, write down exactly what you can do to make your workspace(s) as pleasant, functional, and supportive as possible.

If you write in more than one location, where have you done your best writing? Your most productive writing? Your poorest or least productive writing? Note down this information.

Now turn to your writing schedule. On what day of the week have you been most productive and efficient, or have you done your best work? What time of day has worked best for you? Have you frequently found it difficult to write (or write well) at certain times? If the interval between writing sessions sometimes differs (e.g., if you write Mondays, Thursdays, and Fridays, as opposed to every day or each Thursday), what interval seems to precede your best or most productive writing? Again, jot down your answers for later reference.

Next, look at your writing habits. These might include a pre-writing ritual, the background music you play as you write, the refreshments (or lack of them) you keep nearby, how you dress for writing, and so on. Have all of these been as helpful and effective as you want them to be? What can be changed, added, or done away with in order to better support your writing? Write down whatever useful ideas you may have.

Consider what you've been reading over the past months. What books and short pieces provided you with the most inspiration and material for your own writing? What writers? What genres? Make a note to focus at least some of your reading in these directions in the future.

Then turn your thoughts to the people who have given you feedback on your work. Which of them have been the most helpful, insightful, and/or inspiring? Whose comments have been the *least* helpful, and perhaps even harmful or discouraging? Write down which critics to seek out and which ones to avoid in the future.

The next part of this step requires your full, thoughtful, and careful attention, so plan to take your time. If you need more than one session to complete it, that's fine.

What you'll do now is look through most or all of what you've written so far: your entire notebook, your finished pieces, and, if you like, your drafts, outlines, and netlines.

Begin by paging through your notebook, reading each entry carefully. Look at your list of things that move you; your collected thoughts and observations; your notes from your dreams and daydreams; the connections and patterns you discovered in Step 7; your working notes for pieces, also from Step 7; and anything else you've chosen to include in your notebook.

Then read through each of your finished pieces carefully, one by one. If you like, look at your early drafts and/or outlines or netlines as well. Read these items in chronological order, from the earliest piece to the most recent one.

As you read through all this material, consider these questions:

- Of all the images, ideas, concerns, emotions, themes, subjects, people, and settings that appear frequently in your work, which are the most vivid, powerful, or effective? Which ones appear repeatedly? Which ones surprise you?
- Do any particular words or phrases show up repeatedly?

- What genres, approaches, and/or styles do you work with most often? Which most excite you? Which have resulted in the most moving and successful pieces?
- What other connections or recurring items do you see in your work that you may not have noticed before?

Write down your responses to these questions on your "Sources of Inspiration" sheet.

As you look through everything, new ideas, images, lines, plots, or other items may emerge for you. By all means write these down as well.

↢

When you've finished reviewing all of your material, take a short break. Then come back and look closely at your "Sources of Inspiration" page.

This page will serve as a blueprint for your future writing. It will provide you with suggestions for enhancing your writing circumstances and your writing process; with a list of the key elements that mean the most to you; and with the techniques, approaches, and forms that will make your writing most vivid and powerful.

Post this "Sources of Inspiration" sheet in a prominent place in your workspace—or tape it to the cover of your notebook. It will serve as a master plan for your writing in the months to come, offering you continual, steady guidance.

As the final part of this step, look back again—briefly, this time—at the most recent piece you've completed, then at the very first finished piece you wrote, and then at the initial entries in your writer's notebook. Compare these items for a few minutes, recalling what you were thinking and feeling as you wrote each one.

Then take a few moments more to appreciate how far you've come and how much you've grown as a writer since you first began this book.

STEP 25

Become Familiar With Common Forms and Terms

This step will familiarize you with the major literary genres and forms, as well as with many of the specialized terms used by writers, editors, critics, writing teachers, and people who work in publishing.

YOUR ASSIGNMENT: Carefully read through all of the definitions and descriptions in this step. Make notes on anything that seems important to you.

It isn't necessary to memorize any of the material in this step. However, keep this book handy so that you can consult it and review any descriptions or definitions whenever you need to.

If you have not written any poetry, and have no plans to write any, then feel free to skip over the sections entitled Poetic Terms and Forms of Poetry.

Major Forms of Writing

Every piece of writing falls into one (or more) of three basic categories: *prose, poetry,* and *scripts. Prose* is written in paragraphs, *poetry* (or *verse*) in lines and stanzas, and *scripts* in dialogue and stage directions (descriptions of settings, situations, and actions to be performed by characters).

Any piece of written work can also be classified as a form of *creative, personal, business, technical, professional,* or *scholarly writing. Creative writing* is writing in any category or genre that has as its primary aim the evoking of emotions. The other types of writing are all forms of prose that primarily convey information and ideas.

99 percent of all writing done in English, and at least 95 percent of all writing published in any language, is prose. There are two general types of prose: *fiction* and *nonfiction*.

There are no hard-and-fast definitions of either of these two literary forms. In general, however, fiction is prose that concerns itself with emotional truths rather than with literal ones; non-fiction is prose that recounts (or is substantially based on) real events. Non-fiction is written and published far more frequently than fiction.

The primary non-fiction form is the *essay*, which is a piece that focuses on a single central topic. Longer essays may focus secondarily on other topics as well. Forms of essays include biography, autobiography, memoir, and family history; news stories, features, editorials, and opinion pieces; reports of all types; personal, philosophical, and political pieces; reviews; and scholarly and professional articles. Virtually every non-fiction book can be viewed as either a single lengthy essay or a collection of shorter essays.

The major forms of fiction are:

The novel. A lengthy work of fiction, usually at least 40,000 words long. A novel normally has one central plot and one or more subplots (secondary plots), which build to a climax and resolution near the book's conclusion.

The novella (or short novel). A mid-length piece of fiction, typically between 20,000 and 40,000 words. Structurally, novellas closely resemble novels, and they usually employ many of the same literary devices. However, novellas tend to contain fewer characters, a simpler central plot, and fewer (or no) subplots.

The short story. A brief piece of fiction, normally 20,000 words or less. Typically, a short story is based on a single plot or event, and involves no more than a handful of characters. (Some stories have only one or two characters.) In its most popular and traditional form, a short story begins with one basic conflict or problem; this conflict worsens, creating a tension that builds, more or less steadily, to a climax; a significant change then occurs in one or more characters, in their circumstances, or in the reader's view of the situation; and a resolution (not necessarily a happy or satisfactory one, however) is reached. Over the past several decades, a variety of alternative structures and approaches for the short story have been developed; today, both traditional and non-traditional short stories are frequently published side by side.

The novelette. A term sometimes used for short stories longer than about 7500 or 10,000 words.

The short-short story. A very brief story (typically of 1000 words or less), often with a surprising or ironic twist at the end. The term is sometimes used to refer to any story briefer than 1500-2000 words.

The boundaries between fiction and non-fiction are—and have always been—rather hazy. Humorous essays, for example, are usually considered non-fiction, even though they may be anything but factual. Some "short stories" are, in fact, accounts of actual events, but they are published as fiction because their emotional content rather than their literal truth stands out as most important. (Furthermore, strange as it sounds, it's sometimes easier to publish some essays as short stories than it is to publish them as non-fiction.)

Other literary forms that straddle the line between fiction and non-fiction include:

The vignette (or *slice of life*, or *study*). A brief fiction or non-fiction piece that focuses on and describes a single occurrence, place, or person. Most vignettes have no climax or resolution.

The docunovel. These books, such as Truman Capote's *In Cold Blood,* Tom Wolfe's *The Electric Kool-Aid Acid Test,* and Norman Mailer's *The Executioner's Song,* document real occurrences in novelistic form, and employ many of the techniques of fiction. Although docunovels are usually based on thorough research, they are not usually 100% factual; in these works, absolute precision sometimes takes a back seat to plotting and literary technique.

Creative prose. 1) A non-fiction work which employs many of the techniques of fiction, or which is intended primarily to move rather than simply inform the reader—e.g., Maxine Hong Kingston's "No Name Woman" or Dylan Thomas's "A Child's Christmas in Wales." The term *creative nonfiction* is synonymous with this definition. 2) A piece of fiction written as if it were an essay—for example, Jorge Luis Borges' "Pierre Menard, Author of *Don Quixote*" or Woody Allen's "Lovborg's Women Considered."

Of the major forms of writing, poetry offers the widest array of specific, well-established approaches. I'll describe a number of these in Forms of Poetry, which begins on page 168.

Most verse written and published today does not have regular rhyme or meter. However, these devices are anything but dead or outmoded; in fact, a significant portion of poetry being published today does make use of regular meter, rhyme, or both. (Most good poems that do not use recurring meter or rhyme do, however, make use of a variety of other poetic techniques.) Both rhymed and unrhymed poetry have been around for many centuries, and it's highly unlikely that either one will ever go out of style.

The *prose poem* is a crossbreed of poetry and prose. A prose poem can be defined in two ways: 1) a very short piece of fiction or non-fiction, usually under five hundred words (and almost always under a thousand), that employs many of the techniques of poetry, especially imagery and sound devices; and 2) A poem in which the traditional lines and stanzas are replaced with paragraphing.

᠀

There are essentially two types of scripts—one traditional, the other modern:

The play. A script written to be performed by one or more actors before a live audience. A *full-length* play consists of two or three acts, and normally takes one to three hours to perform. A *one-act* is a brief play of (usually) forty minutes or less. In any play, each act is made up of one or more *scenes*.

The electronic script. A script, of any length, written for radio, television, film, filmstrip, audio, video or audiovisual production. Although there are occasional live performances of such scripts on radio or TV, most electronic scripts are written to be recorded, edited, and played back later.

🐟

At one of the points where poetry, prose, and scripts all merge we find the *song*, which is a work of prose or poetry (usually) intended to be sung according to a specific musical score. Although many songs rhyme, they don't have to. There are of course hundreds of different types of songs, from opera to rock n' roll to gospel to Tibetan Buddhist chants to advertising jingles. One sub-category of the song is the *libretto*, the words to an opera.

Another literary form that combines poetry, prose, and/or scripts is *performance poetry*, sometimes called *spoken word* or *spoken word art*. This is material (usually but not necessary poetry) written primary to be performed before an audience, rather than read silently by individual readers. Competitions in which multiple writers perform their spoken word material are usually called *slams* or *poetry slams*.

🐟

It's quite possible for a piece to fall into two or more of these different genres at once. For example, a poem can tell a fictional story, or a play can be written in verse.

In publishing, television, film, and the theater, a distinction is often made between *commercial* work and *literary* work (and between commercial and literary publishers). No one has ever adequately clarified the distinction between the two; indeed, many writers—such as Toni Morrison, Umberto Eco, Edgar Allen

Poe, and Mark Twain—clearly fall into both categories. Nevertheless, in general, a piece of writing that is intended to interest a wide audience is typically called commercial, while one whose intended audience is intelligent, sophisticated, and, thus, somewhat limited is usually considered literary.

The distinction is easier to make with publishing companies, magazines, and websites. Copper Canyon Press and Milkweed Editions are clearly literary book publishers, while Evans and Company and Ten Speed Press are just as obviously commercial presses. *New Letters* and *Beloit Poetry Journal* are literary journals, while *Redbook* and *Organic Gardening* are commercial magazines.

General Writing Terms

Acronym. A word (or a non-word read as a word) made up of the initial letters of other words--e.g., NASA (National Aeronautics and Space Administration) or snafu (situation normal—all fouled up).

Active voice (*or active language*). Writing that shows people, groups, organizations, or creatures doing things, as opposed to events simply occurring. The following sentences are in the active voice: *I ate lunch. Audrey delivered the package to Eduardo.* Compare these sentences with those in the *passive voice* (or *passive language*): *Lunch was consumed. A package was delivered to Eduardo by Audrey.* Or, worse, *Delivery of the package was accomplished.*

Advance. Money paid to a writer by a book publisher in advance of (or on) a book's publication, in exchange for the right to publish that book. Like a salesperson's draw against future commissions, an advance is applied against a book's future earnings.

Allegory. A tale in which the characters—and often the setting, central images, and/or plot as well—represent specific things, ideas, or institutions. George Orwell's *Animal Farm* is a modern allegory.

Allusion. A reference in a piece of writing to some familiar person, place, thing, or event.

Ambiguity. Anything that can be understood in more than one way. Used intentionally and carefully, ambiguity can add depth and power to your writing. Confusing or unintentional ambiguity, however, can have precisely the opposite effect.

Anaphora. The deliberate repetition of a word or group of words in successive lines or phrases.

Anthology. A group of short pieces by a variety of authors on a central theme, or around a central premise. Anthologies are usually (though not inevitably) published in book form. Compare with *collection* (see below).

Automatic writing (or *free writing*). Writing down whatever comes into your head, without pausing, editing, or (in some cases) following common rules of English usage.

Bibliography. A list of sources used in the writing of an essay. This list is included for readers' reference at the end of some pieces.

Book proposal (sometimes called *portion and outline*). A package presented to book publishers for the purpose of securing a publication contract for a book that has not yet been completed. Typically, a book proposal consists of one to several finished chapters; a detailed plot synopsis (for fiction) or outline (for nonfiction) of the entire book; a brief overview of the book; an "about the author" page; if appropriate, an introduction and/or a table of contents; and, sometimes, a marketing and publicity plan and/or an audience analysis.

Cadence. The rhythmical flow of language in a literary work, particularly a poem. The term refers primarily to the pattern of accented and unaccented syllables, but also to other sound devices, and to changes in pitch and volume.

cf. An abbreviation meaning *compare with* or *compare to*.

Character. Any person who appears in a literary work. An animal playing a significant role, as in Jack London's *The Call of the Wild* or the Curious George stories, is also considered a character. Fairies, elves, trolls, robots, ghosts, etc. can be characters as well. *Characterization* refers to the creation, use, and development of characters.

Citation. Any reference to the original source of a concept or quotation. Citations can be provided directly within a sentence, in a parenthetical comment, in a *footnote* (see below), or in an *endnote* (see below). To *cite* something is to provide a citation for it.

Cliché. Any trite or overused idea (war is hell), phrase (*It's raining cats and dogs*), or image (the pipe-smoking professor in a jacket with leather elbows). Clichés are instantly recognizable, yet carry little power or meaning.

Climax. The point of greatest conflict or tension in a literary work. A resolution or change of some sort usually occurs simultaneously, or soon afterward. Some literary works have one or more secondary climaxes in addition to a primary one.

Collection. A group of short pieces by a single author published as a group, usually in book form. Compare with *anthology* (see above).

Context. Situation.

Denouement. The final resolution or sorting out of events in a literary work.

Development. The buildup of plot, characters, images, ideas, and other elements in a literary work.

Dialect. A specific variant of a language that has its own vocabulary, intonations, pronunciations, and/or grammar. In various dialects, *Nuts! What rotten weather!* becomes *Uff da! What ishy weather!* or *This weather sucks, man,* or *Oy, weather like this I've never seen.*

Dialog (also spelled *dialogue*). Usually, any verbal exchange between people or characters. Sometimes used to refer to any words spoken by a character, even one person talking to themselves.

Diction. Word choice, over and above considerations of grammar. *I opened the bag containing the lunch that belonged to me* is grammatically correct, but has very poor diction. *I opened my lunch bag* would be far better diction.

Draft. A version of a piece of writing composed more or less from beginning to end. A *first draft* is the first such version; a *second draft* is the second version; and so on. A *final draft* is a finished piece.

e.g. For example.

Ellipsis points (or *ellipsis*). Three or four periods in a row. Used to indicate a pause, a gap (usually in time), or an omission of words. When used at the beginning or end of a passage, an ellipsis indicates a fading in or a trailing off. Normally an ellipsis has three dots; use four dots, however, to indicate the omission of the end of a sentence, the omission of the beginning of the following sentence, or the omission of one or more entire sentences.

Endnote. A piece of ancillary information, or a reference source, placed at the end of a chapter, piece, or book, and indicated in the text by an asterisk (*) or a superscript number (^{3}). Compare with *footnote*, below.

Epiphany. A moment of realization, awakening, or sudden insight. An epiphany can occur for a character, the reader, or both.

Feature (or *feature article*). A substantive article in a magazine, newspaper, newsletter, or website—as opposed to reviews, brief opinion pieces, letters to the editor, etc.

First person. Writing which has *I* as its subject is *first person singular; we* is *first person plural.*

Flashback. A scene that transports the reader out of the main flow of events to an incident, real or fictional, that took place previously.

Focus. A widely-used but potentially-misleading term that can mean point of view, theme, or emphasis, depending on its context. When it's used in relation to your work, it's best to ask to have the word defined.

Footnote. A piece of ancillary information, or a reference source, placed at the bottom of the page, and indicated in the text by an asterisk (*) or a superscript number (^{3}). Compare with *endnote*, above.

Foreshadowing. The use of imagery, dialog, or some other literary device to hint (often subliminally) at future plot developments.

Free writing. See *automatic writing*, above.

Genre. A literary form—e.g., fiction or poetry. The term can also be used to refer to forms within forms, such as short stories and novels, or to specialized categories such as science fiction and westerns. Occasionally, people in publishing will divide fiction into two categories: *genre fiction* (thrillers, male adventure, romance, science fiction, horror, fantasy, and mystery) and *mainstream fiction* (everything else).

Gerund. A verb transformed into a noun by adding *ing* to it, as in *drinking, thinking,* or *having.*

Ghostwriter. Someone who creates a literary work for another person but receives no byline (or, in some cases, receives a secondary byline)—hence the word *ghost.* Many books supposedly written by celebrities, sports figures, and politicians are in fact ghostwritten.

Grammar. Rules of writing. These are distinct from *diction* (see above), or common conventions of a language.

Homonym. A word that sounds exactly like another word, but which has a different meaning, and usually a different spelling as well. Some examples: *stair* and *stare*; *shoe* and *shoo*; *gross* (noun), *gross* (verb), and *gross* (adjective).

House (or *publishing house*). A book publishing company. Can also refer to a specific *imprint* (i.e., product line) at a book publisher. For example, Ballantine, Doubleday, and Crown are all imprints of Random House.

Hyperbole. Deliberate—and usually extreme—exaggeration used to add emphasis. Hyperbole frequently takes the form of a *metaphor* (see below) or *simile* (see below). It is often intentionally humorous, and is normally meant to not be taken literally.

Ibid. Used (mostly in the past) in footnotes (see above), endnotes (see above), and lists of references, this simply means *from the source most recently cited.* It's normally italicized and followed by a page number.

Idiom. Any expression that's widely used but not literally true, logical, or sensible. Examples: *We danced up a storm. I feel like you're feeding me lies. I think I'll take a rain check on that.*

i.e. That is. Here's an example: *Make it easy for editors to contact you—i.e., have an e-mail address, a fax number, and voice mail or an answering machine.*

Image. Any sensory impression or set of such impressions. An image can engage any of the senses, or any combination of two or more. *Imagery* is the use of images.

Imprint. See *house*, above.

Infinitive. Any verb with the word *to* before it—e.g., *to laugh, to eat, to remember,* etc.

Irony. An outcome, result, or occurrence that is exactly the opposite of what was planned, hoped for, or expected. An example: a city dweller moves to the country to be alone, only to find himself visited incessantly by neighbors who feel lonely and isolated. The term also refers to a figure of speech in which the intended meaning is exactly (and deliberately) the opposite of its literal meaning—e.g., saying to a runner as she zooms past, "Good morning, Pokey."

Lead. The opening section (which typically presents a key image, theme, concept, or question) in a piece of prose.

Lyrical. Musical-sounding. Not to be confused with a *lyric poem* (see page 168), or *lyrics,* which are the words to a song.

Op ed piece. An editorial or opinion piece, normally published near the front of a magazine or on the editorial pages of a newspaper.

Meiosis. Deliberate understatement for literary (and often ironic) effect. Example: *Stephen King has enjoyed some success with his horror novels.* Synonymous with *litotes.*

Memoir. 1) Autobiography; 2) Autobiography that focuses on spcific events, people, places, or times in the writer's life. Personal accounts of growing up, building a career, war, natural disaster, or terrorism are typically considered memoir rather than autobiography.

Metafiction. A work of fiction that reveals, explores, or is partly based on the relationship between fiction and its readers. John Barth and Robert Coover have written many metafictions.

Metaphor. A literary device that compares or relates one person, thing, or idea to another, either directly or by implication, through the use of an image. Metaphors are of course not literally true. Example: *Max was a demon on the trading floor.* Compare with *simile* (see below). A metaphor is a type of *trope* (see below).

Metonymy. A *trope* (see below) in which the name of one thing is substituted for another. The sentence *I love Sherman Alexie,* for example, substitutes an author's name for his work. The speaker is saying that they love Alexie's fiction, not that they know and love him as a person.

Mixed metaphor. 1) A metaphor that confuses or inappropriately combines two different images; 2) Two different metaphors carelessly thrown together. Examples: *Sour grapes are not my cup of tea; I was just shooting off my mouth at the messenger.*

Monolog. A speech, of any length, made by one person or character in a literary work. An *interior monolog* (sometimes called an *internal monolog*) is the presentation of one person's extended thoughts or deliberations. Sometimes spelled *monologue.*

Mood. The overall feeling or atmosphere created by a passage, scene, stanza, or piece. Compare with *tone* (see below).

Multiple submission (or *simultaneous submission*). The act of sending the same piece of writing to more than one publication at once.

Narrator. The voice or character in a literary work who relates what occurs. In Bill McKibben's *The Age of Missing Information,* McKibben himself is the narrator; in Mark Twain's "The Notorious Jumping Frog of Calaveras County," the narrator *purports* to be the author, but is in fact a character of the author's creation. A *disembodied narrator* is a narrator who has no specific persona at all; most newspaper articles have such a narrator, as do some poems and fiction pieces, such as Shirley Jackson's "The Lottery." An *omniscient narrator* is a disembodied narrator who has superhuman powers of perception. An omniscient narrator might, for example, describe several characters' innermost thoughts, or relate events that none of the characters could possibly be aware of. Some literary works, such as William Faulkner's *As I Lay Dying*, have several different narrators; others, such as Woody Allen's "The Gossage-Verdebedian Papers" (which is composed entirely of letters between two increasingly-antagonistic chess players), have no narrator at all. *Narration* is the relating of events by a narrator. A *narrative* is a stretch of narration, or a piece composed entirely of narration.

Non sequitur. 1) A phrase that's meaningless or irrelevant— e.g., *Nixon's the one*; 2) Any inference or conclusion that doesn't logically follow from its premises, as in *It may be winter, but I'm going to buy a briefcase.* Non sequiturs (especially political slogans) often sound more meaningful than they genuinely are.

Obscure. 1) Unclear, vague, or ambiguous; 2) Unknown or virtually unknown.

¶. A symbol for the word *paragraph*. Inserted between two sentences, it indicates where a new paragraph should begin. *No ¶* at the beginning of a paragraph is a suggestion or instruction to merge that paragraph with the previous one.

Pacing (also called *pace* or *rate of revelation*). The speed at which events take place in a literary work. If a great deal happens in a few lines or paragraphs, the pacing is rapid; if there is little movement of events for several pages, the pace is relatively slow.

Paraphrase. To restate something in different words, often in condensed form. Used as a noun, a paraphrase is any passage that provides such a restatement.

Parody. A form of humor (and sometimes ridicule) in which a person, event, institution, or thing (e.g., a magazine, or a particular writer's style) is imitated and exaggerated to the point of absurdity.

Parts of speech. The eight basic types of words: **nouns** (*ghost, nose*), **pronouns** (*she, them, him*), **verbs** (*grow, write, be*), **adjectives** (*heavy, bright, the*), **adverbs** (*slowly, happily*), **prepositions** (*near, around*), **conjunctions** (*and, but, for*), and **interjections** (*wow, oops*). Very short adjectives (*the, a, an*) are sometimes called **articles**.

Passive voice. See *active voice*, above.

Pen name. See *pseudonym*, below.

Phonics (or *sonics*). 1) The use of rhyme, meter, and other sound devices, usually in a poem; 2) How a poem (or other literary work) sounds.

Plot. The sequence of events in a literary work. Some works have a central plot and one or more *subplots*, or secondary sequences of events; other pieces have no plots or subplots at all.

Point of view. See *viewpoint*, below.

Protagonist. The central character of a literary work. Some pieces have more than a single protagonist (as in John Steinbeck's *Cannery Row*; others have no protagonist at all (as in Theodore Roethke's poem "Root Cellar").

Pseudonym (or *pen name*). A false name used by an author as a byline.

Publishing house. See *house*, above.

Re. Regarding.

Redundant. Unnecessarily repetitious, as in *unusual and unique* or *"I'm furious!" he shouted angrily.*

Rhetoric. The art and strategy of using language effectively, especially in order to convince or persuade people.

Rhythm. The ebb and flow of sound in a literary work, particularly its pattern of stressed and unstressed syllables. The term is sometimes used to refer to variations in pacing.

Royalty. The percentage of a book's retail or wholesale price (or the portion of a play's ticket price) that goes to the author. A *royalty statement* is a periodic report of these earnings.

SASE. A self-addressed, stamped envelope. Normally sent to an editor along with a manuscript, to be used for their reply.

Satire. A type of humor which pokes fun at a person, idea, thing, or institution, usually by exaggerating one or more of its qualities.

Scene. A clearly-defined portion of a literary work that recounts a single event or sequence of events. Usually a scene takes place in a single location and/or is written from a single point of view. Compare with *setting* (see below).

Second person. Writing which has you as its subject. Examples: *You don't understand. When you see it for yourself, you'll change your mind.* Sometimes the *you* is implied, rather than overtly stated: *Turn around. Stand up. Don't say a word.*

Setting. 1) Location; 2) A description or set of images that establishes a location and its overall atmosphere.

Sic. When quoting someone else, add sic in brackets immediately following any error of fact, grammar, spelling, diction, etc., to indicate that the error is theirs, not yours. Example: *In response, Mr. Flammarion smiled and said, "Hey, that's small tomatoes [sic], honey."*

Simile. A comparison of one person, thing, image, or idea with another, through the use of the word *like* or *as*. Examples: *After three months of dieting, Sue was thin as a reed; They stared at each other, like two cats about to fight, or mate, or both.* Similes are a type of *trope* (see below).

Simultaneous submission. See multiple submission, above.

Slush pile. Manuscripts sent to editors for possible publication, but set aside to receive the least-careful and lowest-priority consideration.

Soliloquy. A monolog spoken by a character in a play, sometimes directly to the audience.

Sonics. See *phonics*, above.

Stet. A proofreading and editing term that means "let it stand as it was." When you've changed something in your writing, and you realize later that the way you previously wrote it works better, simply write "stet" above your change to indicate that the correction should be ignored.

Stereotype. An overly-simple, one-dimensional representation of a person, place, group, or institution.

Stream of consciousness. A writing technique that presents the thoughts of a character as they occur. Stream of consciousness may use standard English or a modified form of English intended to mimic actual thought. Do not confuse with *automatic writing* (see above).

Subplot. See *plot*, above.

Subsidiary rights. The right to publish, produce, record, perform, or otherwise display or distribute a literary work in additional languages, territories, and/or media once it has been initially published or performed.

Symbol. A literary device in which a person, object, image, or event is used to evoke a meaning other than (or in addition to) itself. The use of symbols is called *symbolism*.

Synecdoche. A figure of speech in which a single part or element is used to represent the whole—e.g., when a king is referred to as *the crown*. In another form of synecdoche, a single member of a group is used to represent that entire group. In the sentence *There are fewer June Cleavers today than ever,* June Cleaver serves as a synecdoche for happy, submissive, middle-class housewives.

Synopsis. A compressed narrative description of a literary work. In a work of fiction, the term *plot synopsis* is more common. Synopses may be written in either the first or third person, and in either the past or present tense. In book publishing, a synopsis is often (incorrectly) called an **outline**.

Syntax. Sentence structure.

Tautology. A statement that uses circular reasoning or seeks to prove itself by restating itself. Example: *People believe what they believe.*

Theme. Any important concern, idea, topic, point, or statement in a piece of writing.

Third person. Writing which has *he, she, it,* or *they* as its subject.

Tone. How a piece of writing (or an individual section or passage) sounds. Compare this with *mood* (see above). The tone and mood of a literary work can sometimes differ dramatically; for example, the tone of much of Edward Gorey's work is quite grim, yet the overall mood is usually light-hearted and funny.

Trope. Any word or expression used in a sense other than what is commonly intended. *Metaphor, irony,* and *synecdoche* are all forms of tropes.

Unsolicited manuscripts. Writing sent to editors that they have not specifically asked to see. If an editor knows you and asks you to write something for them, that piece has been solicited.

Usage. Rules and standards for language, including grammar, punctuation, and syntax.

Viewpoint (or *point of view*). The perspective through which events and images are related and/or viewed. A literary work can be written from the viewpoint of one of its characters, its author, a bogus author (i.e., someone who claims to be the author, but is in fact a creation of the author), or a disembodied or omniscient narrator (see *narrator*, above). A single literary work may use one, two, or multiple viewpoints—usually but not necessarily belonging to one or more of its characters. The following sentences, about a character named Henry, are written in the third person, but are nevertheless from Henry's viewpoint: *Henry stopped, knowing he was trapped, and looked frantically in both directions. He had to find a way out.*

Voice. The tone and manner in which a narrator writes and/or speaks.

Poetic Terms

A complete introduction to poetic terminology would require a full book. Indeed, there already exists an excellent volume on the subject, Paul Fussell's *Poetic Meter and Poetic Form.* A good (but shorter) introduction to poetic terms and conventions also appears *The Norton Anthology of Poetry.*

Below is a brief and, of necessity, somewhat less than complete introduction to the most important poetic terms and concepts:

Stanzas are groups of lines separated by a single line of blank vertical space. A stanza can be any length, from one line to an entire poem. The end of each line is called a line-break; the end of each stanza is a **stanza-break**. Each line-break or stanza-break creates a visual pause, but not necessarily an aural one (i.e., one you hear when the poem is read aloud, or that you hear mentally when you read the poem silently).

When a line leads straight into the next without an aural pause, this is called **run-on lines** or (more commonly) **enjambment**. (The two lines are thus said to be **enjambed**.) When an aural pause coincides with the end of a line, the line has what is called an **end-stop**, and is said to be **end-stopped**. A pause *within* a line is called a **caesura**.

A two-line stanza is known as a **couplet**; a three-line stanza, a **tercet** or **triplet**; a four-line stanza, a **quatrain**; a five-line stanza, a **cinquain** or **quintet**; a six-line stanza, a **sextet** or **sestet**; a seven-line stanza, a **septet**; and an eight-line stanza, an **octave**. (Longer stanzas have no formal names.)

Any emphasis on a single syllable is called an **accent** or **stress**. (Such a syllable is thus said to be **accented** or **stressed**.) The pattern of stressed and unstressed syllables within each line of poetry is called **metrics** or **meter**; any group of two or three syllables is known as a **poetic foot**. The metrics of any given line of poetry (except lines containing only a single syllable) are made up of one or more poetic feet.

There are seven different poetic feet. Each represents a different pattern of stressed and/or unstressed syllables:

Iamb (or **iambic foot**): an unstressed syllable followed by a stressed one, as in *hello, Japan, arrange, today*, or *the roof.*

Trochee (or **trochaic foot**): a stressed syllable followed by an unstressed one, as in *baby, stop sign, common*, or *backward.*

Dactyl (or dactylic foot): a stressed syllable followed by two unstressed ones, as in *natural, basketball, superglue,* or *other one.*

Anapest (or anapestic foot): two unstressed syllables followed by a single stressed one, as in *understand, jubilee, in a sense,* or *overwhelm.*

Amphibrach (or **amphibrachic foot**): three syllables—the first unstressed, the second stressed, the third unstressed. Examples: *condition, arrival, my darling, the plumber.*

Spondee (or **spondaic foot**): two stressed syllables in a row, as in *M.D., heartbeat, head nurse,* or *stay calm.*

Pyrrhic (or **pyrrhic foot**): two unstressed syllables in a row. Examples: *by the, in a, so he.*

Note that in some cases a single poetic foot can include two or even three words. In other cases, a single word may be made up of two or more poetic feet; the word *paramecium,* for example, is made up of one pyrrhic and one dactyl. (It's of course possible for certain words to be pronounced or metrically analyzed in more than one way.)

A poetic foot that ends on an accent has **rising meter**; one that ends on an unaccented syllable has **falling meter.**

A line containing only one poetic foot is a line of **monometer**. If a line consists entirely of the same foot repeated twice, it is a line of **dimeter**; a line repeating the same foot three times (and containing no other syllables) is a line of **trimeter**; four times, **tetrameter**; five times, **pentameter**; six times, **hexameter**; and seven times, **heptameter.**

The meter (if any) of a poem reflects the type and number of poetic feet in each line. If each line of a poem contains four dactyls (e.g., *Under the willows we settled our differences*), that poem is written in **dactylic tetrameter**. If the first line of a poem contains three iambs (e.g., *I never thought to look*), that line is composed in **iambic trimeter**. If a line includes two or more different kinds of poetic feet, it is written in **mixed meter.**

Sprung rhythm is a variation of traditional poetic feet in which each foot consists of a single accented syllable plus any number of unaccented ones. When read aloud, however—or when heard mentally during silent reading—each foot takes up the same interval of time. The following line uses a sprung version of iambic tetrameter: *He said I was a fool for showing my rage.*

To **scan** a poem is to identify the type and number of poetic feet in each line. **Scansion** is how a poem scans.

Rhyme is, of course, a repetition of the same sound—either the same vowel sound (as in *do* and *crew*), or the same combination of a vowel sound and a consonant sound (as in *map* and *trap*, or *messy* and *Bessie*, or *tureen* and *the screen*).

When a rhyme occurs in the final syllable of two or more words, this is called **masculine rhyme** or **single rhyme**. When rhyme occurs in the next-to-last syllable, and the final syllable of both words is identical (as in *attention* and *prevention*, or *storage* and *forage*), this is known as **double rhyme** or **feminine rhyme**. When the last two syllables of two or more words are identical, and the rhyme occurs in the syllable before that (as in *nutritional* and *transitional,* or *interrupted* and *so corrupted*), this is referred to as **triple rhyme**. When a rhyme occurs *within* a single line (as in *In the frozen fields my husband wields the scythe*), this is known as **internal rhyme**.

Slant-rhyme (also called **half-rhyme, near-rhyme, imperfect rhyme,** or **off-rhyme**) occurs when either an identical vowel sound or the same consonant sound—but not both—appears in two different words. Examples: *fell* and *whale, murk* and *slack, crafty* and *shifty, ostensible* and *expendable.* Slant-rhyme can also occur when two words end in similar, but not identical, vowel sounds—e.g., *bay* and *see.* Words that rhyme visually but not aurally (as in *bread* and *mead,* or *strafe* and *café*) are said to have **eye rhyme**.

The pattern of rhyme in a poem is called its **rhyme scheme**. Specific rhyme schemes are represented by the first few letters of the alphabet. For example, in a quatrain in which lines one and four rhyme with one another, and lines two and three rhyme with each other (but not with lines one and four), the rhyme scheme would be written ABBA. If lines one and two were to rhyme with each other, and three and four with one another, the rhyme scheme would be AABB; and if all four lines were to rhyme with one another, the rhyme scheme would be AAAA.

Other common—and useful—poetic terms include:

Alliteration. The identical initial sound in two or more words, as in *bat* and *barbecue*, or *crisp* and *crass*. Words do not need to be immediately sequential in order to be alliterative.

Assonance. The repetition of the same vowel sound, as in *better yet, black hat,* or *under the bundle.* Assonance can appear in any syllable(s).

Blank verse. Unrhyming iambic pentameter. Not to be confused with *free verse* (see below).

Canto. A section of a poem, usually numbered.

Consonance. Repetition of the same consonant sound in any syllable or syllables, as in *stepped stealthily, renowned name,* or *gathering throng.* This last example includes two instances of consonance.

Distich. A couplet, usually rhyming, that contains a single complete thought or message.

Free verse. Poetry written without regular rhyme or meter. Good free verse nevertheless makes use of a variety of other poetic techniques; it may also use rhyme and/or meter in an irregular fashion. Do not confuse with *automatic writing* (see page 153) or *blank verse* (see above).

Onomatopoeia. Words and phrases that sound very much like what they mean, as in *crunch, snap, grunt, goop,* and *slush.*

Prosody. The study of patterns of sound, such as meter and rhyme.

Refrain. A recurring line, phrase, group of lines, or stanza in a poem or song.

Forms of Poetry

Poetry does not need to conform to a preset structure; indeed, most of what is written and published today does not. However, there exist several forms of verse that follow clear (and often complex) rules. The best-known of these include:

The ballad. A poem or song that tells a story. Ballads are usually made up of four-line stanzas that rhyme ABCB or ABAB. Compare with *ballade*, immediately below.

The ballade. A poem of three eight-line stanzas, each of which rhymes ABABBCBC, followed by a single four-line stanza (called an *envoy*), which rhymes BCBC. Don't confuse this with a ballad (immediately above). ·

The haiku. A traditional Japanese and Chinese form of verse that lends itself surprisingly well to the English language. A haiku consists of a single stanza of three brief lines. Lines one and three are five syllables each; line two is seven syllables. Traditionally, a haiku does not rhyme, and contains (or focuses on) a single vivid or surprising image, often involving nature. Although American haiku writers have often strayed from the naturalistic tradition, they have not modified the 5/7/5 structure.

The lyric. A short poem expressing a single emotion, narrated by a single speaker. Not to be confused with *lyrics*, which are the words to a song. Compare with *lyrical* (see page 157).

The rondel. A poem of fourteen lines that rhymes ABBAABABABBAAB. Line one is identical to lines seven and thirteen; line two is identical to lines eight and fourteen.

The sestina. A rigidly-structured form of verse containing six six-line stanzas and one final three-line stanza (or *envoy*). Stanzas two through five all conform to the following pattern: the final word in line one is the same as the final word in line six of the previous stanza; the last word in line two repeats the last word in line one of the previous stanza; the final word in line three repeats the final word in line five of the prior stanza; the last word in the fourth line is the same as the last word in the previous stanza's second line; in line five, the last word repeats the last word of the prior stanza's fourth line; and the final word in line six is the same as the last word in the third line of the previous stanza. The concluding three-line stanza contains all six of these repeated words. A sestina normally does not rhyme.

The sonnet. A fourteen-line poem, usually in iambic pentameter, which follows a rhyme scheme such as ABBAABBACDECDE, ABBAABBACDCDCD, ABABCDCDEFEFGG, or ABABBCBCCD-CDEE. A sonnet normally contains one to four stanzas.

The villanelle. A complex form of verse made up of six stanzas. The first five stanzas are each composed of three lines that rhyme ABA; the sixth stanza consists of four lines, and usually rhymes ABAA. Lines one, six, twelve, and eighteen are identical; line three is distinctly different from line one, but identical with lines nine, fifteen, and nineteen.

It is quite permissible to vary any of these forms to suit your purposes. For example, you might write a poem that's similar to a sonnet, but which contains eighteen lines instead of fourteen, or which employs hexameter instead of pentameter.

All of the forms described above continue to be practiced and published today, though in some cases (e.g., the rondel) not widely.

_____

At this stage you've accumulated a good deal of writing experience; you've begun a self-designed reading program; you've become acquainted with a variety of important terms and forms; you've built up a storehouse of material to work with in the future; and you've assembled a collection of completed pieces which all bear your byline.

Now you're ready to get your best work into the hands of readers. Turn to Part 5 and I'll show you how to send your work to editors for publication.

PART 5

Getting Published

STEP 26

Prepare a Manuscript for Submission to Editors

So far, you've been writing for three very important reasons: to please yourself; to grow steadily more skilled as a writer; and to create the very best pieces you can. Now I'd like to suggest a fourth reason: to share your insights, observations, and talents with an audience. The single best way to do this, of course, is to publish your work.

I don't mean to suggest that you *have* to publish (or try to publish) what you've written. Publishing your work is always an option, never an obligation. But it's important that, as a writer, you at least know how to get your best work published.

You need to be selective, of course. Don't rush to publish everything you write. When you feel a piece is finished, ask yourself, "Is this piece good enough to be published, or is it really just a useful exercise?" If it's an exercise, file it away. But if you feel that others will find it moving and rewarding, don't let modesty or fear hold you back. Get that piece into the hands of some editors.

Do keep in mind, however, that the publishing world is not always reasonable, honest, or fair. A great deal of good writing gets turned down by editors for arbitrary, silly, and even downright stupid reasons. Mark Twain's hyperbole about publishers—that there are two types of publishers: crooks and incompetents—still rings true (as hyperbole) today. Nevertheless, the fact remains that a well-written piece is always far more likely to be published than one that has obvious weaknesses.

YOUR ASSIGNMENT: If you're primarily a prose writer, look through the finished pieces you've written so far, and ask yourself which ones are strong enough to merit publication. Then select from this group the *one* piece of prose that you believe is the best you've written.

If you're primarily a poet, pick out your best *five* short poems; or, if some of your poems are more than two or three pages long, select eight to twelve pages of your best work. All of these poems should be submitted together, in a single batch. (If your best work is a single poem longer than five pages, then submit only this one piece.)

If you genuinely feel that you haven't yet written a publishable story or essay, or a sufficient amount of publishable poetry, then don't go any further with this step right now. Instead, continue to focus your attention on writing as well as you can, and create several more new pieces by repeating Steps 7–21. Later, when you feel you've written some material that's worth publishing, return to this step. (Don't let fear, resistance, or modesty steer you away from this step forever, though. Once you've finished a dozen prose pieces, or two dozen poems, your option to postpone this step has expired; submit your best work to a group of editors, even if you don't feel very confident about the material.)

It's essential that each manuscript you submit be prepared according to the accepted standards of the publishing industry. These standards are arbitrary, of course, but they help to make the process of publishing a little easier and more consistent for everyone. Properly preparing a manuscript is like dressing up for a job interview; it makes an appropriate first impression, and it conveys the message that you know what's expected of you.

Prepare your manuscript according to the following guidelines:

Use plain, white, medium-weight (16 to 20 lb.) 8½×11 inch paper. Use paper without lines, holes, or rounded corners.

Standard photocopying or computer paper works very well, and is available for about $3–4 a ream (500 sheets). Use only one side of each page; leave the other side blank.

Print out your manuscript on a laser printer; high-end ink-jet printers are acceptable, but laser is better. Use only black ink for your text. (If your piece requires color illustrations, these can of course be included in color.) Pick a typeface that's clear and easy to read, such as Arial, Courier, Times Roman, Tahoma, Garamond, or Verdana. Avoid any ornate or unusual typefaces. Your font should be no smaller than 10 point and no larger than 14. One exception: you may, if you wish, use a larger size for your title on your first page. Your manuscript should of course look clean and attractive, and be as error-free as possible.

Set margins of about an inch on the bottom, left, and right. Leave the right margin unjustified (uneven). On all pages but the first, your text should begin about 1½ inches below the top edge of the page.

Each page except the first should have what is called a *page heading* on the far right, about a half inch below the top edge. Each heading includes the page number and some key words that quickly identify your piece—e.g., its complete title, a significant portion of the title (such as *Mockingbird* for *To Kill a Mockingbird*), your full or last name, or some reasonable combination. Begin your text three or four lines below each page heading. (Note: the first page of each manuscript should *not* have a page heading or page number.)

Things *not* to include in your manuscript include: your social security number (your editor will ask for it if they need it); the rights you wish to sell (these are normally negotiable); and a copyright notice (such a notice isn't necessary or useful until the piece is published).

Do not bind or staple your manuscript; instead, use a large paper clip—or, for manuscripts of over 15 pages, a butterfly clamp (a large paper clip shaped a bit like a butterfly).

Special instructions for most prose manuscripts:

Use the upper-left-hand corner of page one to provide editors with the following personal information, all of which should be typed single-spaced, flush left:

Line 1: your name (not your pen-name, if you're using one).

Line 2: your street address or post office box.

Line 3: your city, state or province, and zip or postal code.

Line 4: your e-mail address (if you have more than one, list only one).

Lines 5-8: your phone number(s). If you have both work and home phones, include both, and indicate which is which; if you have a cell phone and/or a fax number, include these. Each number goes on a separate line.

In the upper right of this initial page, opposite your name, flush right, type "About ____ words"; fill in the blank with an appropriate rounded number. If your piece is 4000 words or shorter, round the word-count to the nearest 100 words; if it's 4000 to 10,000 words, round it to the nearest 500 words; and if it's longer still, round it to the nearest 1000 words.

In the exact center of this first page, type your title, either in all capital letters or in both capitals and lower case letters. Drop down two single-spaced lines, then type your byline (e.g., "by Scott Edelstein"). If you are using a pseudonym, use it here, but not at the top of the page.

Drop down four more single-spaced lines and begin typing the text of your piece. This text should be double-spaced from beginning to end.

This unnumbered first page is considered page 1, and the page the follows is page 2.

If you like, include with your manuscript a floppy disk or CD that contains an electronic file of your piece. This should be saved in Rich Text Format (also called RTF) for maximum compatibility; any word processing program can save files in RTF. This disk should be placed in an envelope on which you have written or typed "DISK VERSION." Tuck the envelope inside the paper clip, between your cover letter and the first page of your manuscript. (Exception: do not include a disk with poetry submissions.)

Two sample pages of a prose manuscript appear on pages 178–9.

Special instructions for prose manuscripts to be sent to scholarly publications:

A scholarly publication is any magazine, newspaper, anthology, or website published more or less exclusively for scholars and scholar/practitioners in a particular field. Examples include *Philosophy and Public Affairs*, *The Journal of Transpersonal Psychology*, *The New England Journal of Medicine*, *College Composition and Communication*, *Art History*, and *Animal Genetics*. The following are *not* scholarly publications: *The Chronicle of Higher Education*, college and university alumni magazines, and literary journals (including those published by colleges and universities).

Prose pieces intended for scholarly publications should be formatted somewhat differently. Here are the differences:

Your initial page should be a separate cover page, which should not include any text from your piece. (This text should begin at the top of the following page, which is considered page one. The unnumbered cover page is thus "page zero.")

The top 45 percent of your cover page should be blank. Your title should appear in the exact center of the page, with your byline (with the word "by" omitted) two single-spaced lines below it. Your contact information (address, e-mail address, phone numbers, etc.) should appear two inches *below* your byline, single spaced and centered, and your word count should appear an inch or so below that, also centered.

If you are employed by (or enrolled in) a college or university, use your college address, phone number, fax number, and/or e-

mail address when possible. If you have no such academic affilia-
tion but work for a professional organization that's connected with
the academic field, use your work address, phone number, etc.

Use your real name in your byline. If you wish your piece
published under a pseudonym, do not use it or mention it. *After
your piece has been accepted for publication*, contact the editor
and ask them to publish it under your pen name.

A sample cover page for these prose manuscripts appears on
page 180.

Special guidelines for poetry manuscripts:

Each poem, no matter how short, should be typed on a separate page and considered a separate manuscript. Longer poems
may of course run more than one page.

With the exception of the upper right of the first page, each
manuscript should be either single-spaced (double-spaced
between stanzas) or 1½-spaced (triple- or 2½-spaced between
stanzas). You may use more space between stanzas if you wish to
create a larger conceptual break.

In the upper left or the upper right of the first page, type the
following information:

Line 1: Your name (not your pen-name, if you wish to use one).

Line 2: Your street address or post office box.

Line 3: Your city, state or province, and zip or postal code.

Line 4: your e-mail address (if you have more than one, list
only one).

Lines 5-8: your phone number(s). If you have both work and
home phones, include both, and indicate which is which; if you
have a cell phone and/or a fax number, include these. Each number goes on a separate line.

If your manuscript is single-spaced, use single-spacing for
this information; if your poem is 1½-spaced, use either single

spacing or 1½ spacing. If you're placing this information in the upper left, type it flush left against the left-hand margin; if you're putting it in the upper right, type it flush left against an imaginary margin about three inches from the right edge of the page.

Drop down four to six single-spaced lines. Type the title of your poem in all capitals, or in bold and/or slightly larger upper and lower case letters, flush left. Do *not* add a byline. Then drop down another three to four single-spaced lines and begin your poem.

If you wish your piece published under a pseudonym, do not use it or mention it. After your poem has been accepted for publication, contact the editor and ask them to publish it under your pen name.

Clip all of your poems together into one batch with a single paper clip or butterfly clamp. Don't use staples.

Don't include a floppy disk or CD with poetry submissions.

A sample poetry manuscript appears on pages 181–2.

You now have a carefully-written, well-prepared, neat-looking manuscript ready to be sent out to editors. Your main concern now is which editors are most likely to appreciate and publish your writing. In the next step, you'll learn how to discover for yourself which editors and publications will be the very best bets for your work.

Sample pages prose manuscript

Scott Edelstein
3947 Excelsior Blvd., Suite 121
Minneapolis, MN   55416
952-928-1922
952-928-3756 FAX
scott@scottedelstein.com

About 5200 words

Gifts and Blessings

by Scott Edelstein

The footsteps paused outside their apartment door. Jacek froze, holding the lit match tightly.

"Light the candles," his mother said. "You'll burn your fingers."

"There's someone at the door," Jacek said. The footsteps had made him forget how the blessing began. He stared at the flame creeping up the match, feeling small and stupid.

"If whoever's out in the hall wants us, he'll knock," his father said. "Blow it out and start again, before you set the tablecloth on fire."

Jacek carefully puckered his lips, but before he could exhale, Anna had leaned forward and blown out the flame. "Hurry up, Jacek," she said. "Don't make a big production out of it. All year you've been begging Papa to let you light the candles, so light

Edelstein/2

them already."

Jacek took another match from the box and scraped it hard against

the graphite. It lit with a loud sucking noise, and he carefully lifted it to the closest wick.

He began chanting: "*Baruch ata adonai—*"

There was a sharp, hard knock on the door, and the burning match fell from Jacek's

fingers onto the linen tablecloth. Anna covered it at once with the ashtray to put out the

flame, then uncovered it again and plucked it from the table. The flame had left a tiny

black and brown spot.

"I told you seven years old is too young for lighting the candles," said his mother.

"You couldn't have let him bless the bread instead? Anna, get the door."

His sister pushed back her chair noisily and left the kitchen, smoothing her hair and

tucking in her blouse. A moment later he heard the door open, and a strange male voice

said, "Are you Mrs. Ehrlich?"

There was a pause before Anna said slowly, "No. I'm her daughter."

"Are your parents home?"

There was an even longer silence before Anna said flatly, "They're eating dinner."

"May I come in, please? I'd like to speak with them."

"Papa!" Anna shouted in a high, sharp voice. "Come to the door, please."

Footsteps echoes from the entryway as Jacek's father got up from the table. He

had gotten only halfway across the room when a figure filled the kitchen doorway.

He was the biggest man Jacek had ever seen up close, and he was wearing a

brown soldier's uniform. The top of his head, covered with short yellow hair, came close to

the top of the doorway. His shoulders were wide and his belly, large and round, stretched

Sample prose manuscript for scholarly publication

One Cent per Word, $300 per Book
Making a Living as a Writer in Early Nineteenth
Century America

Scott Edelstein

Graduate Liberal Studies Program
Hamline University
1536 Hewitt Avenue
St. Paul, MN 55104
952-928-1922
952-928-3756 (fax)
scott@scottedelstein.com

About 4200 words

Sample poetry manuscript

John Sorrell
Box 285
Saltspring Island, BC V8K 2V9
openings@uniserve.com
250-537-1532

Mason's Change

My ears tingle. Through the trees back behind us,
another twig snaps. Jim swings that big deer gun
around in a shot, then runs with a shout
how he got it, he got it. At last
I catch up, and there,
breathless, we see.

The doctor said just one more rib down, poor girl
might have stood a fair chance. I knew that face
from school, but we'd hardly spoken. The hole
deep. Dark. They lowered her in, Jim
locked tight behind his bedroom door,
white window blind pulled tight.

Three years since then, out for bass last week, I caught
a rusty box. Inside, savings bonds, big fistfuls, dripped
against Jim's college list we'd worked on one night, hunched

Sample poetry manuscript (second page)

Sorrell • Mason's Change • page 2

close to our campfire, each star he'd marked sharp there
blurred ghostly now, drowned. Shut back, bubbling quiet,
it all sank down through the dark again.

Nice day, I say. Face turned, he pumps. Black gas hose
clenched tight, tighter yet, pumps more, till at last
the bell dings. Tank full. Time up. Christ,
three years. Not a word. Not a glance.
Just my change, clinking dull here,
still warm from his hands.

STEP 27

Research Potential Markets for Your Work

Each piece of writing has its own unique audience. Readers who will be moved by your poem about your brother's death are not necessarily the same people who will appreciate your short story about the battle of Appomattox. Doctors, parents, teenagers, and Catholic priests might all be interested in reading an essay on birth control, but each group is going to want a different approach and perspective.

Each publication has its own unique audience, too—as well as its own slant, its own approach, and its own agenda. *Science News* is not going to print a murder mystery or an article on how to buy stocks, no matter how well-written either piece may be. And although *Ms., Cosmopolitan,* and *Ladies' Home Journal* are all women's magazines, only *Ladies' Home Journal* is going to publish "The World's Best Christmas Cookie Recipes," and only *Ms.* is going to publish an article on women's rights in Somalia.

What does all this mean for you? Simply this: Getting published isn't just a matter of writing well. *For each story, poem, or essay that you hope to publish, you must locate those publications that print the type of material you've written, and that reach the same readers your piece seeks to reach.* Thus it's essential that you do some careful market research to determine which publications (or *markets*) are right for your work. And, unless you are writing entirely in a single limited field, such as how-to gardening features or science fiction stories, you will probably need to do a new round of research for each new piece that you write.

The only truly effective way to research potential markets is to examine a wide array of publications (and/or their websites), one at a time. There are no short cuts. You may, if you like, read through the *market listings* (brief descriptions of what sorts of writing various publications are looking for) in writers' periodicals and websites, and in reference books such as *Writer's Market*. However, many of these listings are incomplete, misleading, or out of date. These resources *can* help you to establish an initial pool of promising-sounding publications; but you must then look through an issue or two of each one, and/or browse though its website carefully, in order to really get a feel for what it publishes. (One exception: *Writer's Market* contains an excellent, and generally very reliable, list of trade publications: magazines, websites, and newsletters written for members of specific professions—e.g., farmers, dry cleaners, management consultants, etc.)

Keep in mind that many of the pieces you write may be appropriate for more than one type of market. For example, a short story about two women who raced a dogsled across Minnesota might be published in a literary magazine, a general-interest magazine (e.g., *Harper's*), a women's magazine, a sports magazine, a large newspaper's Sunday supplement, an outdoor publication, or a magazine that focuses on Minnesota or the Upper Midwest. An essay on a professional tennis player's breast cancer might be appropriate for a health magazine, a women's publication, a tennis or sports magazine, or the health and lifestyle pages of many newspapers.

YOUR ASSIGNMENT: Begin by making a written list of those publications (including online publications) that you think might be interested in the manuscript (or group of poems) you've selected. If you like, use writers' magazines, websites, newsletters, and/or reference books to come up with ideas. If you have some doubts about certain publications, write down their names anyway; you'll have your chance to check out each one thoroughly later in this step.

Also spend some time browsing the web for possible markets for your work. Start by doing a Google search of obvious key words—for example, "dog magazine," "poetry journal," "mystery stories," etc. Often websites for publications in a particular field will have links to similar publications' sites, or will at least mention them. When you find a publication that looks interesting, note its editorial address (which is usually different from its subscription and advertising addresses) and the name of the appropriate editor. (More on this topic in a moment.) This will give you a pool of additional possibilities.

Then visit a large newsstand or bookstore—one with the widest selection of magazines and newspapers that you can find. If there is no such store near you, it's worth making a trip to the nearest city to find one. Bring pens, paper, and your list of possible markets with you.

Browse at length among the various publications. Take your time; five extra minutes of research now can save you an hour of wasted effort later. Spend at least 45 minutes looking around. Look carefully at all the publications in the pool of possibilities you created from your research of websites, writers' magazines and reference books. Also look for other appropriate publications that you may not have encountered before.

If a publication looks like it might be appropriate for your work, scan its table of contents and at least one or two of the pieces in it. Ask yourself these questions:

- Whom does this publication try to reach?
- What slant, focus, or perspective does it have?
- What themes, subjects, and genres appear in it?
- How long are the pieces that it publishes? How long is the shortest piece in it? The longest?

Whenever a publication strikes you as an appropriate place to publish your work, write down its title, its editorial address (remember, this may differ from its subscription and advertising addresses), its phone number, and the name of the proper editor to approach. In magazines and newsletters, you'll find all of this information on the contents page, or within half a dozen pages before or after it. In newspapers, this information normally appears on one of the editorial pages, which are usually near the rear of the first or second section. Sometimes the name of the section editor appears on the first page of the appropriate section.

If you need to look at a publication in more detail, either purchase it (it's a tax deductible business expense) or make a note to look at it more carefully when you visit a good library.

And it's to a large library—the larger, the better—that you'll proceed next. This should be the main public library of a large city, or the main library of a large university, or both. (If your work is appropriate for publication in literary magazines, it's a good idea to visit both.) Follow the same procedure that you went through in the newsstand or bookstore. Focus your attention only on current and recent issues; anything older than six months won't give you much of a sense of what that publication is doing *now*. Again, take your time; spend a couple of hours if needed.

If you can't find a publication that you're looking for, ask a librarian to order the two most recent issues for you through inter-library loan. Or, if you prefer, get the publication's address and phone number from a reference librarian, and order a copy of the most recent issue directly from the publisher. Another option: call the publisher, explain that you're a writer interested in submitting some of your work, and ask for a copy of the most recent issue. Some publishers will send you a copy at no charge; at worst, you'll be asked to mail a written request and a check.

Continue your market research—visiting more libraries and/or stores if necessary—until you've drawn up a list of at least ten publications that you feel will be interested in your work. Why ten? Because getting published is a game of percentages: the more copies of a piece you send out, the better your chances are of getting it published. Sending out ten copies of a piece to ten editors is really a minimum; approaching 12–20 editors at once is better.

One important—but often overlooked—part of market research is getting the names of the right editors to approach. Locating the right editor is essential; if you send your work to the wrong person, or simply to "Editor" or "Fiction Editor," chances are good that it will get placed in what's called the *slush pile* —the group of manuscripts earmarked to receive the least serious and most cursory consideration. For this reason, *always* send your work to a particular editor *by name*. Here are some useful guidelines for identifying the proper editors:

For magazines and newsletters (including online publications):

As you examine the list of editors and other staff members near the front of the publication, look for an appropriate department editor (e.g., the editor for travel, sports, fiction, poetry, etc.). Send your work to this person unless the publication has a very large circulation (e.g., if it's a magazine such as *Playboy, Vanity Fair, Vogue,* etc.)—in which case send your work to the appropriate assistant or associate department editor.

If editors are not assigned to specific departments or genres, send your work to the editor or editor-in-chief (the titles are synonymous); if no such title is listed, send your submission to the person holding the position of publisher. One exception: in the case of large-circulation magazines such as *Harper's* or *The Atlantic,* step down a notch; write to an assistant or associate editor (or, if no such title is listed, a senior or managing editor) instead.

For newspapers only:

In the case of large and medium-size papers, send your work to the appropriate department or section editor. Smaller papers— such as arts and entertainment papers, suburban papers, neighborhood papers, and other newspapers published no more than twice a week—may not have department editors at all. In this case, send your work to the feature editor. If there's no feature editor, send it to the editor or editor-in-chief. And if no such position is listed, send your work to the publisher.

If two or more editors of a publication share the same job title, pick one at random, or follow your hunch.

You can always, of course, simply call up any publication and say, "Can you tell me who's your current _____ editor?" However, some of the larger publication may refuse to give out this information—or, worse, the operator may tell you, "Just send it to Feature Editor" or "Address it to Poetry Editor." *Never* do this, though—the person is trying to direct your manuscript into the slush pile.

Another option is to check the most recent edition of one of these reference works, both of which are available in some large libraries:

- *The Working Press of the Nation.* Volume 1 contains a good list of editors for most of the newspapers published in North America; Volume 2 contains an equally good list of magazine and newsletter editors.
- *Bacon's Magazine Directory.* Contains an excellent list of editors for thousands of magazines.
- *Bacon's Newspaper Directory.* Contains a very good list of editors for virtually every newspaper in the United States.

Here are some other general tips on doing market research for your writing:

- It's not terribly hard to get published in most big-city newspapers. But the larger a circulation a *magazine or website* has, or the more well-known it is, the tougher it is to get published in it. As a result, magazines such as *The Atlantic, The Saturday Evening Post, Redbook, Cosmopolitan, Playboy,* and *The Paris Review* rarely publish work by new writers. For this reason, I suggest sending your submissions primarily to local, regional, special-interest (e.g., *Outside, Dog Fancy, Ski, Minnesota Women's Press, Alfred Hitchcock Mystery Magazine,* etc.), and other small and mid-size publications. After you've published four or five pieces in these publications, your chances of getting published in big-name magazines goes up considerably.

- Beware of display ads in writers' publications and the Yellow Pages that begin "Get Published," "Authors Wanted," or "To the Author in Search of a Publisher." These ads are usually for *vanity presses*—book publishers that print virtually anything that comes their way, so long as the author is willing to pay a hefty fee for the privilege. Vanity presses produce decent-looking books, but bookstores rarely order them (would you order books from a publisher that prints everything it receives, no matter how badly written?). This means that almost every vanity press book is a huge financial flop for the author.
- Some other scams and schemes to avoid:

  ➤ "Copublishing" arrangements, in which the author and the publisher supposedly split the cost of publishing the author's work, but which usually turns out to be vanity publishing under another name

  ➤ Magazines, literary agents, and book publishers that charge writers a fee to have their work considered for publication.

  ➤ Literary contests that exist primarily to suck up contestants' entry fees.

  ➤ "Book doctors" and other schemers who promise that they will make your work publishable if you pay them a hefty fee to edit or revise it.

  ➤ Poetry anthologies (most of which run display ads in writers' publications) that accept for publication virtually any poem they receive, no matter how inept, so long as it is under 15 or 20 lines long. Each anthology contains thousands of poems, and authors can get copies only by ordering them at the "special" price of $40–60.

Do not participate in any of these schemes. They serve no one but their schemers, and they may cost you a good deal of money and heartache.

At this point you've got a manuscript ready to submit, a willingness (in fact, I hope, an eagerness) to send it out, and a list of people and publications to submit it to. You're ready to package up your work and send it on its way. In the next step you'll learn how to present your work to editors most professionally and effectively.

STEP 28

Submit a Manuscript for Publication

In this step you'll bring together everything you've learned from all of the previous steps. You'll assemble ten complete submission packages, and you'll put these in the mail to editors at ten different publications. Along the way, you'll also do some more writing.

Each submission package should contain either a single work of prose (of any length), or five to seven short poems totaling no more than 12 pages.

If you have longer poems, you may submit fewer than five, for a total of up to 12 pages. You may submit only a single poem if it is longer than five pages, or if you are sending it to a special-interest publication that only occasionally publishes poetry (e.g., if you're sending a poem about sailing to a sailing magazine).

An essential part of any submission package is a *cover letter* — a brief letter introducing your work (and, if appropriate, yourself as well). Writing a good cover letter usually isn't difficult; it's largely a matter of following a standard form and a few simple rules.

Your cover letter should be brief and to the point—normally no more than three or four short paragraphs on a single page. The writing should be clear, concise, and businesslike. Consider a cover letter a communication between professionals, *not* a sales pitch or advertisement. Prepare each cover letter in standard business letter form, using black ink, single spacing, a standard font and type size, and a letter-quality printer (laser if at all possible).

The first paragraph of your cover letter should describe your submission *very* briefly, in a single phrase or sentence. For example:

- I'm pleased to send you "The Painted Moon," a short story set in contemporary Zimbabwe.
- I've enclosed a copy of "Borrowing 101," a parents' guide to the Department of Education's higher education loans.
- I wanted you to have a chance to see my most recent feature, "Santa on a Surfboard," a factual but not terribly reverent look at Christmas in Australia.
- Enclosed are several of my newest poems, "In Hiding," "Hanging Up," "Telepathy," "The Open Range," and "Lost in Riyadh."

If your submission is a piece of non-fiction intended primarily to help or instruct readers, you may, if you wish, explain why your piece is useful or important—but don't take more than a few sentences to do it. For example:

Last summer, Congress made some new changes in how—and how much—it will allow parents to borrow for their kids' college educations. On the surface, the new regulations appear to be more liberal, permitting more borrowing and a more flexible payback period. But these policies could saddle the next generation of college students with burdensome debts that they'll still be paying back as they approach middle age. The enclosed article, "Borrowing 101," takes a hard-nosed look at the U.S. Department of Education's new regulations, and focuses on the specific ways in which these changes will help and hinder college students.

Your next paragraph should—again, very briefly—present a small amount of information about you. This information must either 1) establish you as an experienced and serious writer, 2) relate your background or experience to your submission in some relevant way, or 3) both. For instance:

- These poems are based on the three years I spent as a child in an Algiers orphanage, which bore little relation to the orphanages here in North America.
- I've been writing fiction for the past two years and have been enjoying your magazine for well over a decade.
- I've published short pieces in two area newspapers, and have an essay forthcoming in the magazine *Speakeasy*.

You must tell the truth about yourself, of course—though there's nothing wrong with putting the most positive spin on it. (For example, the "pieces in two area newspapers" mentioned above might be brief book reviews in two neighborhood publications.) Don't mention anything that will sound trivial or irrelevant, like your honorable mention in the local Kiwanis Club's writing competition.

If you have nothing relevant to say about yourself—and this is often the case with newer writers—then omit this paragraph from your letter entirely.

Your final paragraph is your chance to add a few details pertaining to your submission. First, let the editor know that you're enclosing a self-addressed, stamped envelope (or SASE)—and, if appropriate, a floppy disk or CD containing an electronic file of the piece. Your SASE will normally be a regular business-size envelope with a single stamp on it. Include in this paragraph instructions to recycle or destroy any manuscript that the editor does not wish to publish. Conclude this paragraph with a friendly closing statement of no longer than one sentence.

Print out a separate letter for each editor; never use a photocopied form letter. Each cover letter should of course be addressed to the appropriate editor *by name*, not by title (e.g., write to Nathan Maxwell—not to Associate Editor, or to Nathan Maxwell, Associate Editor). Use the editor's first name in your salutation—i.e., *Dear Chris, Dear Pedro,* or *Dear Louisa.* In the 21st century, publishing has become a very informal business; most editors will appreciate the informality, and few will object to it.

Two sample cover letters appear on pages 195-6.

You'll notice that I've said nothing about sending work to editors by e-mail. That's because the great majority of unsolicited manuscripts—that is, manuscripts that writers send to editors on their own initiative—are still sent to editors via regular mail. For a couple of years, before spam and viruses became overwhelming, writers often sent manuscripts to editors by e-mail. Now, however, it's less common; and some network administrators require employees in their companies not to do it.

As a general rule, then, you are better off sending manuscripts in hard copy. If you like, add a copy on a floppy disk or CD (except in the case of poetry). The two obvious exceptions to this rule are 1) computer and high-tech publications and 2) online publications. Both of these should of course receive all cover letters by e-mail and all manuscripts as attachments. Be sure that your subject line reads "Feature article for possible publication" or something similar, or your manuscript will be considered spam and deleted.

Also avoid sending manuscripts by fax, for two reasons: 1) You can't include a disk or a stamped return envelope with a fax, and 2) Faxed manuscripts can easily get lost, separated, or misplaced.

Once you develop a working relationship with an editor, you typically *will* be asked to send your work as an e-mail attachment or fax. But when you're just starting out, stick with snail mail for sending out most of your work.

One final point: in general, use regular mail for sending your work to editors. Don't use special delivery, registered mail, or courier services. None of these will impress anyone or dramatically speed up delivery (they may even slow it down), and they'll be unnecessarily expensive.

Sample letter #1

3444 Klein St., #12
Milwaukee, WI 53202
414-988-2009 (w), 414-290-0117 (h)
414-290-0128 (FAX)
carlawrites@earthlink.net

November 20, 2004

Tracy Macaulay
Sample Magazine
288 Conklin Ave.
Fort Smith, AR 72903

Dear Tracy:

I'm pleased to send you my newest short story, "Opening Lines,"
which I hope you'll want to use in an upcoming issue. The story
concerns the first meeting of two cousins raised in very different
subcultures; it is set in rural Arkansas, a location that I know has
long been of interest to **Sample.**

I've been writing fiction seriously for well over a year, and have
been a serious reader of **Sample** for at least a decade.

I've enclosed both a hard copy and a computer file of "Opening
Lines," as well as a stamped business-size envelope; if you choose
not to publish this story, simply let me know by letter, and recycle
or dispose of the manuscript copy and disk.

If you have any questions, feel free to call. Enjoy the upcoming holiday.

Sincerely,

Carla McNaughton

Enc.:
"Opening Lines"
SASE

Sample letter #2

23019 Santa Barbara Drive
Evanston, IL 60202
312-224-9971
312-224-8886 FAX
amvalentino@aol.com

December 9, 2004

Jerry Wexler
Travel Editor, *Imaginary Life*
34 Spring Street, Suite 406
St. Paul, MN 55101

Dear Jerry:

Chicago's O'Hare Airport is the busiest in North America and the fourth busiest in the world. Unfortunately, for most travelers, O'Hare is about as familiar as the ruins of Machu Picchu and as easy to deal with as the programming instructions for their VCRs. Indeed, most adult Americans live in secret (if minor) dread of either hearing or having to say the words, "I'm stuck at O'Hare."

The enclosed travel feature, "Surviving O'Hare," is intended to provide relief. It's a user-friendly, hands-on guide to arriving at, leaving from, getting around, eating and drinking in, and generally taming the beast known as O'Hare.

I've been a frequent business traveler—usually in and out of O'Hare—for the past seven years, and have made negotiating that airport something of a personal mission for the last five.

The usual SASE is enclosed, as are both hard copy and disk versions of the feature. If you have any questions—or if you're ever stuck at O'Hare and need some sage advice—give me a call.

Regards,

Alice M. Valentino

YOUR ASSIGNMENT: Begin by writing a strong cover letter according to the guidelines above.

Then assemble ten complete, professional-looking submission packages, one for each of the ten editors and publications you selected in the previous step. Follow these specifications:

Print out or photocopy ten clean photocopies of your manuscript. In the upper left-hand corner, using a paper clip or butterfly clamp, clip together the following items, in this order (from the top down):

- Your cover letter.
- The envelope containing your floppy disk or CD (optional, and for prose manuscripts only).
- Your stamped return envelope.
- Your manuscript.

One exception: if you are sending your work to a publication in another country, *don't* enclose an SASE. Instead, enclose an *unstamped,* self-addressed business envelope and a single *International Reply Coupon.* (IRCs are redeemable for postage in any country in the world, and are available at most large post offices.) In the final paragraph of your cover letter, explain that you're enclosing an IRC.

Slip the whole works—manuscript, cover letter, disk (if appropriate) and SASE—into an envelope large enough to easily accommodate it all. Generally, you should mail your submission, flat and unfolded, in a 9×12 or 10×13 envelope. However, if you have a group of poems that totals six pages or less, you may fold the material in thirds and mail it in a regular business-size envelope. (It will weigh more than an ounce, however, and will thus need additional postage.)

Using a computer printer, neatly print all names, addresses, and return addresses on both your mailing envelope and your SASE. If you use manila envelopes, print out this information on mailing labels, and affix these to the envelopes. Make and save a written list of all the editors and publications you've targeted, including addresses, phone numbers, and the date you mailed each submission.

Mail your work via first class—or, if it exceeds 13 ounces, use either Priority Mail or UPS. If you're sending your work outside the country, use overseas air mail. (Ask about the special "small packet" rate, which is a special rate for small packages sent air mail to certain countries.)

You do not need to copyright your work before submitting it (it is fully protected by copyright law from the moment of its creation), nor do you need to mail a copy to yourself to prove ownership.

When you've got ten packages put together, weigh them, affix sufficient postage to both the outgoing packages and the SASEs, and drop them in the mail.

This practice of sending the same piece to more than one publication at a time is known as making *simultaneous* or *multiple submissions*. Most professional writers follow this practice, which has become the norm in almost every area of publishing. However, there are a few exceptions to this rule. Do *not* send the same piece simultaneously to:

• More than one newspaper with a national or international readership—e.g., *The New York Times, The Los Angeles Times, The Chicago Tribune, USA Today, The Wall Street Journal, The Washington Post* or *The Christian Science Monitor.*
• Two or more big-city newspapers that have significantly overlapping readerships (e.g., the Minneapolis *StarTribune* and the St. Paul *Pioneer Press*).
• Two or more scholarly journals.

Once you've sent out your manuscript, don't wait expectantly by the phone or mailbox. Get on with your life and your writing. Do, however, make a note on your calendar to follow up on any submission that you don't hear about within a reasonable amount of time. Wait 12 weeks for a reply to any prose submission, 16 for poetry.

If you do need to follow up—and you probably will with three or four editors—make a brief, polite, businesslike phone call to each one. Whether you reach them in person or reach their assistant or voice mail, say something like this: "My name is _____. On (date) I sent you a manuscript entitled _____, and I've not yet heard from you regarding it. Please let me know whether you'd like to use it; you've decided to pass on it; it's still waiting to be read; or you've never received it. You can reach me by phone at _____ and by e-mail at _____. Thank you."

If an editor says they have your manuscript but want more time to consider it, say, "No problem. I'd appreciate a response within a month, though."

If you leave a message, don't be surprised if it isn't responded to. I know this seems rude, but the fact is that many editors are too overworked to to return all of their phone calls. So I recommend making no more than one follow-up call to any editor about any submission.

If, after five months have passed, you've still not gotten a yes or no from a particular editor, simply consider the submission lost, ignored, or otherwise dead, and send the manuscript elsewhere. There's no need to withdraw it, or ask the editor to recycle or destroy it, and there's no serious risk that the piece will be stolen and published anyway. (Outside of the film and TV industries, theft of writers' work is extremely rare.)

If all ten editors reject your work, don't feel discouraged. Rejection is an occupational hazard for most writers. I still get rejected most of the time; in fact, much of what I publish gets rejected several times (sometimes dozens of times) before it finds a home. Shrug your shoulders, reward yourself with something you enjoy, and send out your manuscript to ten more editors.

Remember that persistence in the face of rejection often pays off. The more editors that you continue sending a piece to, the more likely it is to be published. I sold this book after receiving rejections from 34 publishers; as a literary agent, I once sold a book after getting it rejected 111 times. Robert Pirsig's bestselling book *Zen and the Art of Motorcycle Maintenance* was rejected 107 times before Morrow offered to publish it. *Chicken Soup for the Soul,* perhaps the best-selling publishing phenomenon of all time (after the Bible) was rejected over 30 times, by all the major publishing houses in the country.

And if an editor wants to use your work, congratulations! See my book *The Busy Writer* for detailed information on negotiating a publication contract.

What if two or more different editors want to publish the same piece? Not a problem. As soon as you and an editor have agreed on the basic terms for using the piece, make a list of the publications you've not yet heard from. Separate these into two groups: those that directly compete with the publication that said yes, and those that don't. (A directly competitive publication is one that reaches many of the same readers. For example, *The Writer* and *Writer's Digest* directly compete, but *Outdoors* and *Yoga Journal* do not.) Write the editor at each directly-competing publication a brief, businesslike note, fax, or e-mail. Explain that you've sold your piece elsewhere, that you're withdrawing it from their consideration, and, if you like, that you hope to send them a new submission shortly. (In the case of poetry, only withdraw the particular poem(s) that have been accepted for publication; tell the editor that the others can remain as live submissions.) This is all you need to do.

As for the non-competing publications, simply sit tight. If an editor at one of them wants to publish your piece, just explain the situation. Because they publish for a very different audience, it's quite possible that they will be willing to publish the piece as well. At worst, they'll explain, politely and regretfully, that they're unwilling to publish something that has been (or will soon be) published elsewhere. You can then thank the editor and tell them that you hope to send them another piece soon. At this point, then, you'll have sold one piece and established good relationships with two different editors. Not bad at all for someone just starting out.

At this stage you've accumulated all the basic knowledge and experience you need to create your best work and to get it into the hands of the right people. Your next step is to gain some more experience, and to begin establishing yourself as a professional.

STEP 29

Think and Act Like a Pro

You've been a practicing writer for some time now. You've written a number of finished pieces, and you've begun to make connections with editors and seek publication of your work. Over the past 28 steps you've come quite a long way.

But it's the policy of this book not to let you rest on your laurels for long—which means that you've got another task ahead of you: becoming a practicing *professional* writer.

According to one common definition, a professional writer is anyone who has had at least one piece accepted for publication by a respectable book, magazine, newspaper, newsletter, or online publisher. But I'm not happy with this definition, because I know of people who have published widely and earned a considerable amount of money from their writing, but whose attitudes and actions are anything but professional.

What *really* makes someone a professional writer is the way in which they approach the art, the craft, and the business of writing. The real pro may or may not have published anything yet, but they bring commitment, energy, integrity, and patience to their writing, and to their personal and professional dealings with others. These are the writers who are most likely to be successful in the long run.

There's no simple set of instructions for becoming a full-fledged professional writer. It's a gradual and ongoing process. But if you do your best to follow the guidelines below, day by day, you'll slowly and steadily become more and more of a pro.

YOUR ASSIGNMENT: Below is a list of practices, principles, and guidelines that most professional writers routinely follow. Read them over carefully; if you like, post them prominently where you write, or add them to your writer's notebook.

As you write and market your work, do your best to practice each one of these principles. At first you may sometimes feel awkward or uncertain, and things may not always go as you would like them to. But as you write each new piece and gain more publishing experience, you'll gradually find yourself becoming more and more of a seasoned pro. This will happen one piece, interaction, submission, business deal, and publication at a time.

- Keep your expectations reasonable—for yourself, for editors, and for other people in publishing.
- Be straightforward and honest in all your business dealings.
- Be civil and businesslike at all times—in person, on the phone, and in letters, faxes, and e-mails—even if the person you're dealing with is not.
- Be clear about what you want, need, and expect.
- Don't expect editors and other publishing people to be perfect. Do expect them to treat you fairly, honestly, and with respect. (If someone doesn't, your best course of action is usually to stop working with them.)
- Live up to whatever commitments you make—and expect editors and publishers to do the same. Meet or beat all deadlines.
- Don't promise what you can't deliver, and never agree to any terms that you're unwilling or unable to fulfill.
- If you can see in advance that you're not going to be able to deliver what you promised by your deadline, let the appropriate person know immediately.
- Ask for, expect, and, if necessary, insist on reasonable fees, terms, and deadlines.

- Stick up for what you feel is appropriate and fair. If necessary, insist on it. Don't let yourself be mistreated.
- If a problem arises, make it known to the appropriate person promptly and straightforwardly.
- When you make a mistake, miss a deadline, or cause a problem, apologize promptly and do what you can to make amends.
- Be willing to make reasonable compromises—but refuse to make unreasonable ones.
- Use proper manuscript form for all submissions, and standard business letter form for all correspondence.
- Accompany all submissions with well-written cover letters.
- Properly cite your source whenever you use anyone else's words or ideas.
- Quote all sources as accurately as possible.
- Don't lie or twist the truth in any piece of writing intended to be factual. Be as accurate as you can.
- When doing research for a piece of writing, be as thorough, as careful, and as detailed as necessary.
- Present your credentials truthfully and accurately, but in the most positive light.
- Set up a workable filing system, so that you can easily save and retrieve important documents.
- Keep at least one backup copy of everything you write. Ideally, keep three copies—one on your hard drive, a backup on a floppy disk or CD or flash drive, and a paper copy in a file.
- Send a manuscript to editors only when you feel it's genuinely worthy of publication, and in the best shape you can get it.
- Do proper market research for any piece you plan to submit for publication. As necessary, do new market research for each piece you write.
- Follow up submissions that have not been responded to within 12 weeks for prose, and within 16 for poetry.
- Read every publication contract thoroughly, negotiate it carefully, and save it in a location that's easy to access and remember.

- Always make clear, unambiguous agreements—preferably written ones—to cover the publication of your work. If you do make an oral agreement, jot down the terms as you talk; then promptly send your editor a letter, fax, or e-mail that details those terms. Add something like this: "This is my understanding of what we've agreed to; if your understanding is different, please let me know promptly."
- Always try to be paid on the signing of your publication contract, or on the acceptance of your finished manuscript. Try to avoid delaying payment until publication. One good compromise: set the payment date for a specific number of days—e.g., 30, 60, etc.—beyond signing or acceptance. The sooner, the better, of course.
- Never agree to anything you find unacceptable. If a publisher isn't willing to negotiate a fair, reasonable deal, it's better to have no deal at all.
- Keep accurate records of all of your submissions, acceptances, and publications. Keep these records together in a submission book or special file.
- Keep an accurate, ongoing account of all your business expenses. (These are normally tax-deductible on your Schedule C. If you have little or no writing income, these deductions can usually be used to reduce your total income from other sources.)
- Don't be afraid to try new topics, genres, forms, approaches, or markets. If a new or unusual (but worthwhile) opportunity presents itself, go for it.
- Be patient and persistent. The people who succeed in the writing business are those who keep at it for years—often in the face of setbacks and rejection.
- Never threaten a lawsuit except as a next-to-last resort. (The final resort, of course, is actually suing.)
- Never throw away anything you write.
- Never pay anyone to publish your work—unless you've become your own publisher and you've hired a printer.
- Write as well as you can at all times.

In order to stay sane, a writing professional needs to keep rejection in perspective. Here are some things to keep in mind as you market your work:

• Virtually all writers have their work rejected sometimes, and most have it rejected frequently. Whether we like it or not, rejection is an inevitable part of being a professional writer.

• Never take rejection personally. *Your piece* is being rejected, not you. Any rejection reflects only on the work you've submitted, not on your overall ability or promise as a writer.

• There are dozens of reasons why a piece can be rejected, and most of these have nothing to do with the quality of the work itself. Publications change their focuses or policies; editors get fired; pieces scheduled for publication get pulled at the last minute when an extra full-page ad comes in; two very similar pieces land on an editor's desk at the same time; and so on and on.

• What one editor will despise, another may adore. I've had pieces published that were previously rejected with rude, angry, and insulting comments.

• Don't let rejection shake your faith in a piece, or in yourself. If you believe in something you've written, keep sending it out— dozens of times, if necessary—until it's accepted. It's not uncommon for something to be accepted for publication after 20, 50, or even 100 rejections.

• Take editors' comments in rejection letters with a large dose of salt. Editors are not always good critics, and their comments are often written hastily and without much thought.

• If an editor rejects your piece but says positive or encouraging things about it, send them something else you've written. And if they tell you that your piece came close, consider rewriting it and sending them the rewrite.

• Never tell an editor in a cover letter that a piece has been rejected before.

• Never write or call editors to argue the merits of a piece they've rejected. Instead, use your energy to send the manuscript to several other publications.

- If an editor turns down a piece, then leaves their job, feel free to send the same piece to their successor. (One writer I know sold a short story to a major magazine after it had been rejected twice by two of the editor's predecessors.)
- If one department editor at a publication says no to your piece, consider sending to send it to a different department editor at that same publication. For instance, if the lifestyle editor at a major newspaper rejects your humorous essay on arguing with teenagers, try sending it to the editor of the paper's Sunday magazine.
- Ease the sting of rejection by promising yourself something you enjoy—your favorite dish, a walk in the woods, a night out—every time a piece gets rejected. *Always* live up to this promise. This creates an automatic win/win scenario: if you're rejected, you do something you enjoy; if you're accepted, you get published. (And, if you like, you can still treat yourself.)
- Some writers deal with rejection by responding to it immediately. Within two days (or one day, or eight hours) of receiving any rejection, they get the piece back out to another editor.
- Some writers do the opposite: they send out a huge batch of submissions all at once, then don't worry about sending out more for several weeks, or even months. If rejections come in, they simply note their arrival, and forget about getting the piece back in circulation until the day of the next scheduled submission blitz.

Once you've become a working professional writer, your primary task is to keep growing. In the final step in this book, you'll look to the future, and to your continued growth and success as a writer.

STEP 30

Build Your Writing Career—and Continue to Grow as a Writer

This final step builds on everything you've done so far, from jotting things down in your notebook to maintaining the highest standards of professionalism. It involves planning your future as a writer, and working to steadily expand your range, your recognition, your income, and your impact on readers.

It's possible to complete this step in a cursory fashion over a period of a few months, at which point you'll have completed this book's entire program. But this step isn't really meant to be finished and then forgotten. It's meant to be put into practice continuously, over and over, as you become ever more able and successful as a writer.

YOUR ASSIGNMENT: First, take an hour or two to look back at how and where you started as a writer, the steps you took as you built your writing career, and where you are now. Review all the progress you made along the way. Look back at the early entries in your notebook and the first one or two pieces that you completed; compare these to what you're writing now. Then compliment yourself on all that you've learned, all the skills that you've developed, and all the results you've achieved over the course of the first 29 steps.

Now turn from the past to the future. In the months and years to come, you'll repeatedly draw from everything you've learned from the 30 steps in this book. Whenever you feel the need or desire, return to any step that seems appropriate. Reread it and, if necessary, repeat the activity associated with that step.

To help support your continued growth as a writer, and as a practicing professional, also do the following:

- Keep writing regularly, according to a manageable and supportive schedule. If possible, gradually increase the time you spend writing.
- Continue to take time to observe, think, and meditate—and to write down images, observations, and ideas in your notebook.
- Review the material in your notebook on a regular basis, and use it to inform and generate new stories, poems, and/or essays.
- Submit your work to editors on a regular basis. Send each publishable piece to at least 10 editors at a time. Keep each manuscript in circulation until it sells.
- Work on longer and more ambitious pieces—perhaps even a book, or a stage play, or a TV or film script.
- Keep reading the work of writers you admire. Take note of how they do what they do, and learn from them.
- Attend public readings by writers whose work interests you.
- Once you've got enough writing experience under your belt, contact the organizers of a reading series to see about giving a reading yourself.
- Find other people who can serve as useful critics for your work in progress.
- If the company and/or criticism of other writers is important to you, join a writers' critiquing group. If you can't find one that you like, start your own.
- Join the National Writers Union, and/or one or more professional writers' organizations (Science Fiction and Fantasy Writers of America, the Society of Children's Book Writers and Illustrators, the Poetry Society of America, etc.).
- Once you've published a few non-fiction pieces, pitch some ideas for assignments to editors of magazines, newspapers,

and/or websites. (Writers usually pitch assignment ideas by letter, but if you've built up an ongoing relationship with an editor, feel free to use the phone or e-mail instead.) Under this arrangement, you sign a contract to write a specific non-fiction piece by a mutually-determined deadline for an agreed-upon fee. Once you have enough experience and publications behind you, some editors start approach *you* with assignment ideas.

- Consider other ways to build your writing career: suggest a regular column to a magazine, newspaper, newsletter, website, or syndicate; sell your services as a writer to businesses and non-profits; apply for jobs as a salaried writer or editor; or come up with your own writing-related entrepreneurial venture.
- Get yourself some business cards. Keep these simple in design (unless you also do design work, in which case they should be gorgeous). Your cards should include only your name, address, phone and fax numbers, e-mail address, and a brief title or description, such as "Writer" or "Literary Services" or "Writing and Editing."
- Have professional letterhead, envelopes, and address labels printed—or run them yourself on your printer. Keep these simple, like your business card.
- Buy and use some basic business gear: a daily planner or appointment book; a postage scale (for weighing outgoing packages); and a fax machine and fax line. If you conduct in-person interviews for your writing, get a portable tape recorder as well.
- Above all, enjoy yourself.

☙

Throughout this book, I've done my best to give you all the tools you need to start writing; keep writing; steadily improve your writing; publish your writing; and, ultimately, become a professional writer of the highest caliber.

I'd be pleased to receive e-mails from anyone who has been helped by this book—especially those of you who have become successful professional writers. I'm also happy to receive general comments, criticisms, and suggestions for future editions. Write to me at scott@scottedelstein.com or visit my web site at www.helpingwriters.com.

I've enjoyed serving as a guide on your journey as writer. May this journey be a steady source of satisfaction and success for many years to come.

APPENDIX

A Writer's Reality Check
An Invaluable Tool for Writers

Some of what you will be told about your writing by writing teachers, editors, friends, and family will be nonsense at best and b.s. at worst. This isn't an accusation or a tale of woe; it's simply a fact, and an unavoidable part of being a writer.

In fact, since we writers are ourselves fallible human beings, some of the things we write—and some of the things we tell ourselves about our writing—will also, on occasion, be nonsense.

A Writer's Reality Check is a practical, quick-reference guide to the most common sorts of nonsense and b.s. you're likely to hear from others—and from yourself.

There's a separate section for nonsense from each of the following sources:

- Writing teachers
- Editors
- Friends and family
- Your own writing
- Your own thinking

Most importantly, *A Writer's Reality Check* also provides specific, practical guidance for responding appropriately to each type of nonsense from each different source.

Detecting Nonsense from Writing Teachers

TYPE OF NONSENSE	PURPOSE OF NONSENSE
Insisting that you write in one particular way (usually just like they do).	1) To make you into a clone of them. 2) To make your writing trendier and, thus, in their mind, more publishable.
Critiquing your personality instead of your writing.	To make you feel small and them feel big.
Focusing only on your piece's weaknesses or problems, and saying little or nothing about its strengths and/or potential.	1) Same as above. 2) To express and reinforce their own negative outlook on life.
Treating grammar, punctuation, and other technical concerns as more important than your piece's emotional power, overall effect, and structure.	1) To express their own hard-edged, black-and-white approach to life. 2) To express their frustration with writers' (or your own) lack of basic skills.
Telling you to find another profession, or that you don't have what it takes to be a writer.	1) To make you feel small and them feel big. 2) To express their dislike for you or your writing.

EXAMPLE(S)	SITUATIONS WHERE YOU ARE LIKELY TO ENCOUNTER IT	RECOMMENDED RESPONSE(S)
"This is out of style now." "Read the following writers and emulate them."	Graduate and advanced undergraduate creative writing programs, especially prestigious ones.	Follow your own vision. If necessary, find a different teacher or writing program.
"Only and angry and frustrated person would write something like this."	Writing workshops and classes.	Say, "Let's look closely at the piece itself, because that's where I can learn the most." If necessary, switch teachers.
"Needs lots of work. Weak characters, over-complex plot, dull language. Not one of your best efforts."	Any close work with a writing teacher.	Ask to meet with the teacher. At the meeting, ask what, specifically, you can do to make the piece work better.
"Don't you even know how to use a semi-colon?" "C+. This would have gotten an A- if you'd paid more attention to grammar and usage."	Any close work with a writing teacher.	Edit and proofread more carefully. If necessary, have a friend or editor edit you, too. Tell yourself that you have a life, but your teacher may not.
"I just can't see you making it as a professional writer." "It's a very tough business. Go into real estate or dentistry instead."	Any close work with a writing teacher.	Don't argue. Remind yourself that Ernest Hemingway was told exactly the same thing by his creative writing teacher.

Detecting Nonsense from Editors

TYPE OF NONSENSE	PURPOSE OF NONSENSE
Vague or mealy-mouthed rejection of your work.	1) To save the time and trouble of providing a thoughtful response. 2) To mollify argumentative or defensive writers.
Stonewalling when negotiating a publication agreement.	1) To get you to drop a particular request or demand. 2) To get the most from you for the least cost.
Trying to pay you nothing for your work, even though the publication does pay some writers, and can afford to pay you.	To get the most from you for the least cost. ,
Assuming that their (or their readers', or publication's, or company's) experience is universal.	1) To express and reinforce their own limited views and perspectives. 2) To get your quick acquiescence without discussion.
Vague or incomprehensible requests for revision.	To improve the piece in question. *(This is good.)*
Aggressiveness, condescension, or mean-spiritedness. *(Rare.)*	To make them feel big and you small. *(Usually a personal agenda, unrelated to their job.)*
Accusing you of being unprofessional. *(Rare.)*	To shame and browbeat you into being exploited.

EXAMPLE(S)	SITUATIONS WHERE YOU ARE LIKELY TO ENCOUNTER IT	RECOMMENDED RESPONSE(S)
"It's not what we're looking for right now." "It doesn't suit our needs at this time." "We can't find a place for it."	Rejection letters (particularly form letters)—primarily those from well-known or prestigious publications.	Translate it to "No, thanks." Work hard to build your writing skills and get published.
"We've never done that before." "I'd need to ask my boss. She's out of town until Friday." "No one has ever asked for that."	Negotiations on publication contracts.	Call the editor's bluff: "I'd like to have that nevertheless. Please ask your boss when she's back."
"We're a small (or religious, or academic, or specialty) operation." "We don't usually pay writers."	Negotiations on publication contracts.	"Have you ever paid any of your writers? You have? How much? Okay, shall we do that amount?"
"Humor doesn't sell." "People don't want to read things like this anymore." "Add some sex. Sex sells."	Rejection letters; requests for revision.	Rejection letters: send your piece elsewhere. Revision requests: agree to reasonable requests only.
"It needs more vibe." "Sweeten up the café scene."	Requests for revision.	Ask persistently for more specific guidance.
"You're wasting my time." "In my lexicon, 'rewrite' means 'improve.'"	Any encounter.	The first time, call the person on their behavior. The second time, contact their boss.
"That's out of the question. No serious writer would ever ask for that."	Negotiations on publication contracts.	Insist on fair terms; if you don't get them, walk away.

Detecting Nonsense from Friends and Family

TYPE OF NONSENSE	PURPOSE OF NONSENSE
Lack of confidence in your ability as a writer.	To protect themselves from disappointment, and/or from being called foolish by others.
Thinking that writing—and writing success—come easily.	To support their own subconscious view that life is (or can be) easy and painless.
Complete and unexamined adoration for everything you write.	To express their love for you; to reinforce their view of you as special. *(These are good things.)*
Belief that writing can't be a serious, decently-paying profession.	1) Concern for your (and your family's) financial well-being. 2) To reinforce their belief that you're unrealistic.
Ignorance about how much most writers earn.	Undervaluing: see the item immediately above. Overvaluing: see item 2 in this column.
Ignorance about the process of getting published.	1) To help you succeed. *(This is good.)* 2) To express and reinforce their view of you as lazy, risk-averse, unassertive, or uncreative.

EXAMPLE(S)	PEOPLE YOU'RE MOST LIKELY TO HEAR IT FROM	RECOMMENDED RESPONSE(S)
"Are you sure this is a productive way to spend your time?" "Typing away again? You've been at it almost two hours."	Parents and spouses.	Don't argue or defend yourself. Work hard to build your skills and get published.
"Why don't you write some bestsellers, like that Stephen King?"	Everyone except other writers.	"Writing's actually a fairly tough business. Stephen King was poor for years."
"Everything you write is so wonderful." "I love it just as it is. Don't change a thing."	Spouses, partners, wannabe spouses and partners, and best friends. Occasionally parents.	Thank them. Also get regular feedback from someone who is both trustworthy and impartial.
"Writing's a nice hobby, but you've got bills to pay. Dry cleaning, now there's a solid business."	Spouses and parents.	"Many thousands of writers make over $50,000 a year." Work hard to build skills and get published.
"Writers don't make any money, do they?" "Wow, you're a published writer, just like John Grisham! You're going to be rich."	Everyone except other writers.	"Writers are like most people. Some are rich; some are poor. Most full-time writers are middle class."
"You need to grab editors' attention. Have it delivered by somebody in an ape costume." "Send it to Oprah. Maybe she can help."	Everyone except other writers.	Laugh and thank them for their ideas. "Lots of people have tried that already. It doesn't work."

Detecting Nonsense in Your Own Writing

TYPE OF NONSENSE	PURPOSE OF NONSENSE
Writing in universals and generalities.	To sound profound. *(It doesn't.)*
Providing judgments instead of important sensory details.	1) To synopsize key information. 2) To tell readers how to feel.
Providing wads of exposition instead of action.	To avoid the work of showing full-fledged events.
Providing wads of dialog or monolog instead of action.	As above.
Beginning with an almost-immediate flashback.	As above.
Using stereotypes.	To avoid the work of showing full-fledged people.
Using reverse stereotypes.	As above.
Being deliberately obscure or unclear; using unnecessarily high-falutin language.	To impress people. *(It has the opposite effect.)*
Using clichés.	To avoid the work of creating fresh language and images.
Using passive language.	To sound more formal and official. *(It actually sounds pompous and dorky.)*
Cutesieness.	To amuse and entice kids. *(It makes most kids and adults gag.)*

Nonsense appears most commonly in early drafts, where its presence is both common and expected; however, it should never appear in a finished piece. Your task is to recognize the nonsense in your writing and replace it with language that is clear, honest, authentic, and the result of real work instead of shortcuts.

EXAMPLE(S)

"Love is like a rose."
"Sorrow often keeps desire at bay, but desire typically increases sorrow—a truth that Yumiko was slowly comprehending."

"It was a truly outstanding experience."
"She had a unique personality that had a lasting effect on everyone she met."

"David had been a lab tech for nine years, during which he earned a master's degree in chemistry and met and married his wife Laura. David's work at the lab led to his volunteering at the county hospital, where he met many fascinating people."

"Well, David," said Laura, "we've been together now for six years, during which we've bought a house and a car and a boat together and begun to raise two adorable children."

"Latisha stared into her brother's eyes. She knew he was angry with her, just like he had been six months earlier when she had wrecked his car. He had nearly fainted when he saw the crumbled front end. 'Jesus, Tish!' he had shouted, 'can't you take care of anything?'"

"Henri had two interests in life: sex and fixing things. He liked lonely women with problems, so that he could merge the two activities."

"Henri had two primary interests in life: shopping and feeling cherished by his wife."

"The tension between experience and concept can only be heightened, never eased, through language."
"Kareem and Janice perambulated through the verdant greenery until they reached the vicinity of her vehicle."

"When Josie saw what Johann had done to the room, she nearly had a cow."
"Oy," said Sheldon, "it's so hot out a person could plotz."

"A decision was made regarding this proposal on the morning of January 19."
"Football was picked by the group as its sport of choice."

"Gosh," thought Selma Squirrel, "if I can't find my spectacles, how will I find the path to Harley Hedgehog's house? I know! I'll ask Karla Kangaroo to put me in her pouch and take me there!"

Detecting Nonsense in Your Own Thinking

TYPE OF NONSENSE	PURPOSE OF NONSENSE
Compulsive self-doubt.	To express and reinforce an old, half-believed image of yourself as untalented or incapable.
Excessive fear of rejection or failure.	To protect yourself from future pain. *(This strategy will not work, however.)*
Judging yourself and your work too quickly.	1) To avoid future failure. 2) To be able to let go of writing and take up something else.
Believing that any result is 100% your doing, or that good writing inevitably results in publication.	To express and reinforce your desire to control everything you encounter. *(Such efforts naturally fail.)*
Avoiding revision or editing.	1) To avoid some potentially-hard work. 2) To get published faster.
Treating editors as anything other than equals.	To express and maintain your self-image as inexperienced or unworthy or lacking knowledge.
Fear of asking for what you want, or what's fair, in a publishing contract.	1) To avoid losing the deal. 2) To avoid being told "no."

EXAMPLE(S)	SITUATIONS WHERE YOU ARE LIKELY TO ENCOUNTER IT	RECOMMENDED RESPONSE(S)
"Who am I to think I can write?" "I don't know how to get started." "I doubt I have any talent."	1) When you first start out as a writer. 2) When you begin a new piece. 3) When you're stuck in the middle of a piece you're writing.	Consider these thoughts to be mental muzak. Let them play on in the background while you keep building your writing skills.
"I don't dare send out my work. If the editors all say no, I'll be mortified and ashamed."	During your first few months as a writer, before you've actually accumulated at least 50 rejections.	Submit lots of copies of lots of pieces to editors. Experience will banish the fear.
"I'll never be able to write like Isabel Allende. I might as well quit now." "I still haven't published anything. Face it, I'm a failure."	When you face rejection, doubt, difficulty, or disappointment during your first two years as a writer.	Force yourself to write for two years before doing a serious self-evaluation. Keep writing regularly until then.
"Every editor so far has rejected my work. I must be doing something wrong."	When you've been rejected repeatedly, especially in a short span of time, during your first two years as a writer.	Remind yourself that life is always uncertain, and that most of it is beyond your (and anyone's) control.
"I think I'll send the rough version to editors and see if anyone bites."	When you're impatient to get published (or impatient in general).	Slow down! Don't send it out yet. Do all the work it needs first.
"I'd better do just what the editor says: after all, he's a pro." "It would be presumptuous to call her directly."	1) Negotiations on publication agreements. 2) When editors request revisions.	Remind yourself repeatedly that you and editors are equal business partners—and both human.
"I'm just starting out, so I should accept whatever terms the editor offers me."	Negotiations on publication agreements.	Take a deep breath and ask. The risk of losing the deal is small

ABOUT THE AUTHOR

Scott Edelstein is best-known as the author of books that inspire and empower writers, including *100 Things Every Writer Needs to Know* (Perigee Books), *The Busy Writer* (Writer's Digest Books), and *The No-Experience-Necessary Writer's Course* (Scarborough House). He has also published several books for college students and their parents, as well as several ghostwritten titles on a variety of subjects.

Over a hundred of Scott's short stories and articles have been published in a wide range of publications, including *Glamour, Essence, The Artist's Magazine, Ellery Queen Mystery Magazine, Single Parent, Campus Life, Docket, Artlines,* and, of course, *The Writer, Writer's Digest,* and *Writer's Yearbook.*

Scott has been a professional writer for over 30 years, as well as a book, magazine, and newspaper editor; a newspaper and magazine journalist; a freelance writer for many businesses and non-profits; a literary agent; an arts reviewer; a columnist for two writers' magazines; and a writing and publishing consultant. He also teaches in the MFA in writing and Master of Arts in Liberal Studies programs at Hamline University in St. Paul, Minnesota. He lives in Minneapolis, where he splits his professional time among work on several book projects; teaching; and consulting with other writers on marketing their work and talents, building careers, and turning their inspiration into finished material. For more information, visit Scott's website, www.helpingwriters.com, or e-mail him at scott@scottedelstein.com.